James Allen
On F1 – 2009:
A Revolutionary Year

James Allen
On F1 – 2009:
A Revolutionary Year

Photography by Darren Heath

SPEED MERCHANTS LIMITED

First published in 2009
by Speed Merchants Ltd

Cataloguing in Publication Data is available from the
British Library

ISBN: 978-0-9564187-0-8

www.jamesallenonf1.com

Printed and bound in England by CPI Antony Rowe,
Chippenham, Wiltshire

Contents

Foreword
by ROSS BRAWN
WORLD CHAMPION TEAM OWNER 2009

It was a very eventful year for Formula 1 and a very special year for Brawn GP. What made it so special was the contrast between where we were over the winter and where we finished the season. In my career I have never known anything like it.

The efforts of the team over the winter to work as hard as they did and be committed as they were, not knowing if they had a future, were possibly unique, as were the efforts everyone made over the year.

We had a sensational first half of the season and a tough second half. Everyone caught us up, we had a dip in form, Jenson had never led a world championship before, all sorts of factors came in. But we came good in the end.

We are the second smallest team in Formula 1 and we have won the world championships and we are proud and worthy champions.

The real measure will be how we can go on from here. In many ways our success makes us more determined not to slip back. But I don't think we will disgrace ourselves next year, we will have a good car and I think F1 is going to evolve to suit teams of the size of Brawn and Williams. The way restrictions are going to come in is going to suit our team so I'm optimistic for the future.

James Allen on F1 is the insider's website. James always has a good perspective on what is happening in our sport. I like the fact that his site doesn't get involved in the tittle-tattle, but focuses on the racing and what is happening with the teams.

My family are huge fans and it is the site they always go to first of all. They will often ring me up to tell me that James has been saying this, that or the other…

To my Mother and Father for all their support over the years.

Introduction

This is the inside story of an extraordinary season in Formula 1. In my 20 years in the sport I cannot recall another like it.

People say F1 is predictable, but we had a totally unpredictable season of racing, with the backmarkers of 2008 coming through to win both the drivers' and constructors' championships. Meanwhile the dominant teams of recent times, McLaren, Ferrari and Renault, all had uncompetitive seasons.

The sense of F1 undergoing a "revolution" was heightened by what happened behind the scenes in 2009, as the teams rebelled against the governing body, FIA, over its plans to introduce a £30 million budget cap for 2010. This impasse took the sport to the brink in June, when the teams announced that they were forming their own breakaway series. A deal was hastily put together to keep the wheels of this huge business successfully moving forwards.

For Jenson Button it was a fantastically positive year. He finally won the drivers' world championship after a chequered 10-year career, while Sebastian Vettel and the Red Bull Racing team each became a major force.

There were also some significant long term moves made behind the scenes, with Ferrari deciding to drop Kimi Raikkonen and hire Fernando Alonso. We were on to that very early on the website and the hunch proved entirely correct. And after 15 seasons as partners, Mercedes began the process of moving away from a minority shareholding in McLaren, towards a controlling interest in Brawn.

These seismic events will have a lasting effect on the sport and Formula 1 has profoundly changed as a result. For a start, costs have been brought under control and the model for the future is smaller teams with fewer staff, lower costs and higher revenues. The influence of the manufacturers is waning; BMW and Toyota pulled out this year, while four new independent teams are scheduled to be on the grid in 2010.

For me personally, 2009 was a year of change. Having been part of the ITV Formula 1 team as a commentator for 12 years, the switch to the BBC as F1 rights holders in the UK gave me a great opportunity to strike out on my own and develop a new media platform, which brings me closer to the fans. I started the *James Allen on F1* website in the form of a blog and over the course of the season, by taking note of readers' comments and those of the many F1 insiders who visit the site, we have evolved it into something that has earned a respected place in the Formula 1 media spectrum.

We had the idea of putting the best of the blogs into a book. It's fascinating to look back and see how the different story threads weave around each other. With the benefit of hindsight you can see how stories developed and why decisions got taken as they did.

Lots of people have helped me a lot with this project, particularly my wife Pip, who has been such a fantastic rock over the years, as many F1 people know. I would really like to thank her for lots of things, but let's just leave it at project managing this book for the moment! Also thanks as ever to my father, Bill, for invaluable help with the manuscript. Thanks too to the many people who helped to put this book together, starting with my wonderful copy editor Kirsty Ennever, to Alan Street at Gardners, Geoff Fisher and all at CPI, Neil Tookey, Andrew Hirsh and Ian Pierce at John Brown for design. Thanks also to all those friends and professionals on the sidelines who have given help and advice.

When I started the *James Allen on F1* website, Luca Menato was a pivotal figure and I want to thank him for the inspiration and for the fabulous banners. I'm indebted to Pete Young, who has worked very hard behind the scenes; and to Darren Heath, who has provided the stunning images. I would also like to thank Lawrence Barretto, Simon Ryley, Henry Calvert, Brian Calvert, Rebecca Willis and Sue Varley. For lots of sound advice I am very grateful to Guy Martin, Alex Salter, Nicola Ibison and Mikah Martin-Cruz. Thanks also to Frederic Layani, Jean Christophe Babin and Herve Bodinier at TAG Heuer.

I'm very fortunate to have built a large network of friends and contacts in the Formula 1 paddock at every level. The administrators, mechanics, team principals, drivers, engineers, journalists and broadcasters to whom I speak all the time, help me to form my view of the sport and I am enormously grateful to them.

Finally, my biggest thanks go to all the many readers of my website at www.jamesallenonf1.com for supporting the site and leaving so many interesting comments.

James Allen
London, November 2009

Chapter One
January 2009

Why it was time for Ron Dennis to stop
16 January 2009

Today's McLaren launch was a quietly confident affair. The team looked composed and calm ahead of what is likely to be a hard fought and chaotic season, with complex new rules and an intense development programme away from the circuit. And then just as the thing was drawing to a close, Ron Dennis, the sport's most successful entrant, goes and lets slip that he's standing down as team principal at the end of February.

It's no great surprise in one sense; he is 61 years old and has been discussing stepping down for some time. He was under pressure from the authorities to quit in 2007 during the Ferrari spying scandal, but he toughed it out, determined to stay in charge until Lewis Hamilton had clinched the world title, which he regarded as the culmination of a project he put in place over 10 years ago.

But Lewis's success in 2008 and the pleasure this gave him seemed to have given him a fresh love of the sport and renewed his motivation. So it was mildly surprising that he chose today to announce that he was finally going to allow his loyal deputy of 20 years, Martin Whitmarsh, to take the top job. As Ron said, they had been sharing the job for a long time anyway and in practical terms Martin had been the boss for a few years, with Ron the figurehead who made his presence felt at race meetings and in the public arena. There will not be much change in the way McLaren goes about its business, although they will probably enjoy better relations with the FIA now that Dennis is out of the way.

I have always said that Dennis is the best and worst thing about McLaren. He had both a positive and a negative effect on his team. He tended to intimidate the team members on the pitwall, for example in China in 2007 when they dithered over leaving Hamilton out on worn tyres. Even senior engineers were afraid to take the initiative some-times when Ron "took over" in a crisis, which he couldn't stop himself from doing.

Whitmarsh will let them get on with it and they will probably be a more effective and more instinctive racing outfit because of that. Last year Dennis drove the mechanics mad at the final race in Brazil by going round urging them to check and double check their work, at the same time repeating "Don't panic!" like Corporal Jones from *Dad's Army*, which naturally had the opposite of the desired effect.

But the passion which can make Dennis such a prickly and wearing character is also a crucial part of the reason why McLaren has been so successful. His relentless attention to detail and obsession about con-stant self-improvement made the team what it is. There is no more professional outfit in the pit lane, but their commitment can verge on the obsessive. I think they can afford to ease off a notch or two on that and will perhaps do even better, but they will certainly miss Ron's passion.

I've had a lot to do with him over the years and have had some very tough experiences and some pleasant ones. He loves jokes, but is better at telling them than listening to them. He's an enigma of a character; extremely complex and yet apparently quite simple, rather like Nigel Mansell – a fellow dyslexic, who similarly seems to feel that he always has something to prove.

Ron needs to impress, needs to establish some superiority; when this was channelled into competitive desire, it made him hugely successful, but at the same time rubbed a lot of people up the wrong way.

As for Whitmarsh, he is a very experienced hand, from an engineering management background. He's the kind of guy who designs a "management matrix", rather than a dirt-under-the-fingernails racer like Dennis or Frank Williams. He's a more laid-back individual than Dennis (but then who isn't?) and a brilliant manager. Of course, you can argue that he could afford to be laid back when he wasn't ulti-mately in charge and we'll see how he changes now that the buck stops with him.

The reason why it is the right time for this change is because the map of F1 is being redrawn and a new generation of bosses is coming through. Stefano Domenicali has taken over from Jean Todt at Ferrari and the formation of the Formula One Teams Association and all the energy that will take from the team principals makes it the right time for Whitmarsh to be given his head. He's a pivotal figure in FOTA and a more suitable character than Dennis to develop and nurture the atmosphere of unity which now prevails between the teams.

Ron will still come to the races, he says, and I'm sure he'll still be on hand for a quote, but I sense that he now wants to rise above it all and become an elder statesman of the sport - even pick up that knighthood, which I know he would regard as the culmination of his life's work.

* * *

Over the winter Bernie Ecclestone was trying hard to sell the idea of awarding gold, silver and bronze medals for the podium finishers in Grands Prix. He was inspired by a visit to the Beijing Olympics the summer before. Controversially the world champion would then be the driver with the most gold medals, not the one with the most points. This idea was not popular with fans and jamesallenonf1.com became a forum for them to voice their dislike of the idea.

* * *

F1 Medals – changing history for the better?
30 January 2009

I have just received an email from the FIA press department with some great research on how F1 history would have been rewritten if Bernie Ecclestone's medals idea had been in place since the start of Formula 1 in 1950. The outcome of the world championship would have been different on 13 occasions.

Felipe Massa would then have won the world title in 2008, which may have inspired the idea. Bernie proposed this idea after he attended the Beijing Olympics last summer.

Ironically the FIA research has revealed that with the medals system the Brabham team under Bernie's tenure would not have won any world championships, losing the 1981 and 1983 titles!

But looking across the span of the years you'd have to say that, with one or two exceptions, the distribution of world championships would have better reflected the calibre of the drivers; Alain Prost would have won five, Ayrton Senna and Jim Clark four and Nigel Mansell three! Also Stirling Moss would have won a world championship. This, I think, would have been a fairer reflection of those drivers' places in F1 history than what we actually have in the record books.

There would have been some losers; Nelson Piquet would have lost all three of his titles. I never thought he was a three-time champion driver anyway, not in the same league as Jackie Stewart, for example. Niki Lauda, though, would have won one instead of three, which would probably have been wrong.

There are some other interesting details, like the fact that Didier Pironi would have won in 1982 instead of Keke Rosberg, which would have been appropriate, Mario Andretti would have won the 1977 title as well as the 1978 and Alan Jones would have won in 1979.

Sport is all about how fate plays with your expectations; sometimes they are fulfilled whilst other times there are spectacular reversals. People expect Roger Federer to win every match and it's a big story when he doesn't, while no one expects Cardiff to get to the FA Cup final today, when teams like Manchester United and Chelsea have wage bills of £70 million a year. That's what makes sport so appealing. It's the only genuine suspense most people have in their lives.

People who really love a sport and go deeply into it, following their passion, have a strong feeling for what is deserved and what is not. However I often feel that F1 fans confuse "likeability" with "talent and ability" and many F1 journalists are guilty of this too. Nigel Mansell, for example, was ridiculed by many of the F1 specialist writers in this country who thought he was a waste of space. But any seasoned engineer will tell you that he was one of the greats. Today a lot of people think Hamilton is overrated because they don't like him, detest his father, or resent his shortcut to the top, but the fact is he's a phenomenon.

For me this research document supports Bernie's argument more than argues against it. I feel quite strongly that many of the results which would be changed under a medals system would have produced the right outcome. Of course if the medal system had been in place at the time, drivers might well have acted differently in races, knowing how the title would be decided.

Against that, the sporting challenge of Hamilton needing to finish fifth in Brazil, sixth would not do it, would have been ruined by the medals plan - Massa would have been cruising towards the title and Lewis would have been adrift and all that fantastic sporting drama would have been lost. Big picture, small picture, which is more important?

This whole question will generate a lot of interesting debate and it's the right time to have that debate because FOTA is working behind the scenes to define the essential DNA of this sport, which in turn is prompting the FIA, who are fairly proactive anyway and Formula One Management, who are less so, to address what F1 is and what we want from it. You, the fans, are part of that process and now is the time to have your say.

Chapter Two
February 2009

Every February FIA president Max Mosley hosts a lunch in London for a few British journalists. It's usually done over two days with the specialists on one day and the Fleet Street contingent another. The concepts outlined here were to set in motion an extraordinary and volatile year for F1 and for Mosley, who would end it no longer the president.

* * *

Lunch with Max Mosley... a busy year ahead
4 February 2009

Today I went along to a lunch thrown by Max Mosley for a small group of journalists at the Poissonnerie de l'Avenue, in South Kensington, London.

The talk was, predictably, about the need for urgent cost cuts, the medals system, prospects for the season ahead, the future of the British Grand Prix, evidence of who set him up in last year's sex scandal and his own future.

On this last point I got the clear impression that he intends to stay on for another term. He has to make his decision by June and as he explained, there is a complicated system whereby prospective candidates have to draw up a list of people for the key jobs. This is a system he initiated in 2005 as it would give him early warning of anyone plotting to stand against him. Wily old fox.

Anyway as he talked, saying that he wasn't sure whether he wanted to do it all again, he made it clear that all the key people want him to run for another term.

I would have thought that he is unlikely to walk away from the job now as the next three years are absolutely critical to the future of F1, with FOTA providing a strong united front for the first time ever and Bernie Ecclestone and CVC very anxious to get everyone signed up beyond 2012 to protect their income stream.

He looked very fit and full of energy, much more so than at times last year. He's going deaf, however and clearly had problems hearing some of the questions. He wasn't playing for thinking time by asking for a repeat, he was genuinely straining to hear. As always he was bitingly sardonic in some of his answers and particularly scathing about the stories put about last week that disgraced former RBS chief exec Sir Fred Goodwin might stand for FIA president this summer.

On cost cutting and the rules for 2010, he was very firm. He said the target is to get budgets right down, to around £50 million. He added that it is regrettable that people will have to lose their jobs in that process, but F1 teams are not in business to employ people for the sake of it. To get budgets down from £300 million to under £100 million cannot be achieved by continuing to employ 1000 people in a team.

Mosley wants to see costs come down so much that a team can run for £50 million and be competitive. He feels that the boards of the main car companies are keen to see costs brought down dramatically and that it needs the FIA to do this because the people who manage the teams on behalf of the manufacturers would not go far enough fast enough.

What he did not say, but I have gleaned privately, is that the FIA has a package to present to FOTA of areas of non-competition, parts of the car which teams would agree not to develop, thus cutting out huge development costs.

Ideally the FIA would like FOTA's agreement on this package, but they do have the option of ramming it through the world council in March or June under the *force majeure* rule – in other words arguing that the economic situation is so desperate in the motor industry that these measures must be taken now or else the whole survival of F1 will be threatened. That will be a major point of contention with FOTA.

On other topics he said medals were not the answer to the overtaking problem and rather seemed to blame the team engineers, who sat on an overtaking working group and came up with the aero rules we have for this year, which he now feels will not improve overtaking. Max feels that slipstreaming is the answer and is getting his people to look further into moveable aerodynamics on the car, which allow the car behind to be faster than the car in front by virtue of being "towed".

He said that Jean Todt's Ferrari contract expires in March and that will mean he loses his seat on the world council, to be replaced by another Ferrari representative (Ferrari get the seat by virtue of having been in F1 the longest). He does not think that Todt will run for FIA president, because he would not want to do so intensive a job unpaid, as the rules insist.

On customer cars he said that as far as the FIA is concerned they are eligible to race this year and said that both Toro Rosso and Force India are expected to field "customer cars" but pointed out that there was some dispute about whether they would qualify as constructors for a share of the TV money.

On the fallout from last year's sex scandal he said that he is now virtually certain who set him up, implied that it was someone in F1 and said that he is waiting for final conclusive proof before he acts. He did not rule out legal action.

Donington not adding up
11 February 2009

I posted last month on Donington, which is due to host the British Grand Prix in July 2010, seventeen months from now. I gave details of a conversation I'd had with Simon Gillett at the Motorsport Business Forum in December. But now some worrying noises are coming out on this story, regarding the circuit's financial position.

The story has run this week in the *Mail*, the *Express* and the *Telegraph*. It refers to the accounts for the year 2007, which were filed at Companies House on 21 January this year, three weeks ago.

They refer to the eye-catching figures of £67 million of debt and losses of £12.7 million. I've seen the accounts and that's definitely what they say, but it's not clear what the debt is made up of, beyond a £16 million bank loan, £4 million of which is guaranteed by Gillett's partner Paul White. White owns a construction business in the Midlands.

The accounts are for the year-end 2007, so they cover the period at the peak of the business cycle and the assets are valued at £55 million. It does not say who valued them. Not much in the property world is worth the same today as it was in 2007. Interestingly, the accounts say that the group meets its day-to-day capital requirements through the bank loan and through support from White. White has indicated that he is willing to go on supporting it, but the auditor notes that he is under no obligation to continue to do so. There is no mention of Gillett guaranteeing any of the loan.

There are warning signs all over the accounts from the independent auditors, who say that they were "not able to obtain or review" documents of financial forecasts or evidence that Donington has binding commitments with providers for the funds required.

This is interesting because Gillett told me last year that he had a deal with IMG and Goldman Sachs on a debenture scheme, which guaranteed him the money. He has said all along that he would reveal details of the debenture scheme at the end of March, so we'll have to wait until then to get the full picture. Bernie Ecclestone has said that he wants to see that the thing is on track by September if the race is to go ahead.

The auditors add that the current downturn creates "uncertainty particularly over a) the level of demand of the group's services and b) the availability of bank and other finance in the foreseeable future".

Gillett told Ian Parkes of PA Sport this week that the whole thing is on track, despite the doubters. He denies that it has the debts being quoted and says that a computer model of the new track facilities will be launched very soon. He said that the 2008 accounts had not been filed yet, but the current stories relate to the most recent set of accounts, for 2007.

All very mysterious. One thing is clear though; Abu Dhabi this ain't.

* * *

Honda had shocked F1 by announcing its withdrawal at the end of 2008. Over the winter team principal Ross Brawn and his management colleagues were fighting to save the team, initially by looking for a buyer, but then deciding to lead a management buy-out. Saved from oblivion at the 11th hour, the team would go on to dominate the 2009 championship.

* * *

The Honda goose chase
16 February 2009

Time is short with the first Grand Prix of 2009 just six weeks away. The former Honda team is in a race against time to be ready. Honda is still paying the bills to keep the team a going concern in case a deal can be done to save them. Honda has a strong desire to see this happen as does Bernie Ecclestone.

Behind the scenes work goes on; the team has had a Mercedes engine and gearbox for some time to get the installation worked out in case the deal to save the team comes off. The problem is that those last minute engine changes often breed reliability problems.

The Honda rescue has become a bit of a soap opera. There has been a lot of misinformation in recent days about the future of the team. A lot of stories have been and continue to be well wide of the mark.

Now a new party has entered the picture, a serious bidder with a strong brand, we are told. I'm in Italy at the moment and there is some speculation here that it could be Virgin.

Virgin is certainly a strong brand, but the company has not done anything in this sport before. They've had a go in bike racing, but why would they want to get involved in F1? Well, maybe they wouldn't, but as we all know they are happy to license their brand to credible third parties, as they have done with Cola, for example. Virgin likes to identify with the outsider, the underdog

I've seen Sir Richard Branson at Grands Prix in the past, always looking pretty impressed at the scale of the thing. Bernie Ecclestone has an interest in keeping this team going and there could well be some complicated deal being worked because at a time when strong brands like Honda, ING and Petrobras are quitting the sport, F1 could do with someone swimming against the tide and showing F1 in a positive light.

Who knows. It seems a strange fit with Virgin, but stranger things have happened.

* * *

Mosley's desire to get costs down was designed to make it possible for new teams to enter the sport and dilute the power of the manufacturers, as well as to ensure that grids would be full if more manufacturer teams withdrew. One such new team was USF1, the brainchild of my long time media colleague Peter Windsor.

* * *

Can the USF1 team get off the ground?
25 February 2009

Peter Windsor and Ken Anderson did a press conference on the US racing channel Speed TV last night with details of their USF1 project.

On the face of it, this is a crazy time to try to get a US-based F1 team off the ground, with a credit crunch, which is biting savagely in America, no US Grand Prix or suitable American driver, and the eternal problem of logistics with most of the races being based in Europe and all points East. Also, whisper it, it's not very green to fly racing cars back and forth across the Atlantic, when you could just as easily be based in Surrey or Oxford.

The key to this initiative is the FIA's move to slash costs and the FOTA's desire to do likewise. Now a team like USF1 knows that it can get an engine and gearbox from a front-running team like McLaren Mercedes or Ferrari for £6.5 million a year. The FIA wants to restrict many other areas of technology and make them available in a similar fashion. The teams are moving slowly towards finding what they consider the right level. If the teams stick to type and resist radical change, then USF1 will really struggle to be anywhere other than the back of the grid with only 100 employees based in the USA.

But if the FIA gets its way and budgets do come down to around £50 million a year and any new technology a team like McLaren comes up with, has to be made available at a capped price to a privateer team, then USF1 will be the first of several new F1 teams having a go, recession or no recession. There are three empty spaces in the pit lane (without Honda) and they will fill up fast if F1 becomes affordable.

F1 still offers a sensational return on investment in terms of advertising spend. A £20 million sponsorship will do far more for global brand awareness than twice that much spent on TV advertising. And if the budgets come down as much as they are talking about, then the business model even allows for profitability.

But we've been here before, seen many a wide-eyed optimist launching in, ultimately to be disappointed. F1 is a bear pit, a piranha tank and the people who've been around a long time and have a lot to protect are not going to make it easy for new boys to come along and make them look foolish.

I know Windsor well, he helped me a lot with the Nigel Mansell autobiography in the 1990s and I've helped him out too in TV. He has always dreamed of his own team and he has been around in F1 long enough to know the harsh realities. There is a hint of fantasy about his project and I do think that his team was rushed into this announcement because of leaks, where they might have liked more time beneath the radar.

But they are now committed to putting two cars on the grid in 2010 and representing the USA. How will they do it? Well, there is quite a silicon valley of motorsport technology in Charlotte and Indianapolis. I've been there and seen it. Most of the car build will be outsourced, and they have the state of the art Wind Shear windtunnel (which Anderson built), just a few miles down the road. You'd also need state of the art F1 technical knowledge; Mike Gascoyne is sitting in Oxfordshire twiddling his thumbs and there are some designers at the Honda base in Brackley who might be available for hire shortly...

Windsor said last night that he has sold a small stake in the team and that they have the capital to start the team and go racing in 2010. He did not give details, but he did have US racing legends Dan Gurney and Mario Andretti on the phone supporting his plans. Andretti sang the praises of his grandson Marco: "If I were to design an F1 driver today, I would design Marco. He learns quickly, he's very much a free spirit. He wants to do it and he'd excel at it."

Sure Marco Andretti and Danica Patrick would get some serious publicity if they were announced as the USF1 drivers next year, but both would have a mountain to climb in terms of learning the tracks with almost no testing allowed. I worked closely with Marco's dad, Michael, when he came over in 1993 and even with all the testing McLaren did in those days, he was struggling to get up to speed.

The buzzword is "skunkworks" – it's what Anderson and Windsor describe as their approach to the F1 project, a small number of very good people, team meetings in Starbucks, the spirit of the 1970s really, using pretty much standard engines and gearboxes. It's Max Mosley's dream too of where F1 should be, whereas Bernie Ecclestone yearns for the highest standards of professionalism, so there is a tension there.

Chapter Three
March 2009

Car makers take a further hammering
4 March 2009

Today's *Financial Times* has some shocking information about the state of the motor industry during this credit crunch. And as F1 is seen as an extension of that industry because of its reliance on, and domination by, the car companies, you need to know about this.

One story says that for most manufacturers, sales of new cars in the United States are down 40-50%. That includes Toyota who have taken a 40% hit.

A little lower down on the page there's a story from Tokyo about how Toyota is seeking a $2 billion bail-out from the Japanese government. The company is facing its first net loss in 60 years.

Meanwhile the number of cars exported from Germany has halved. The bosses of BMW and Mercedes are arguing against government intervention in the car industry because they believe that it will lead to irrational consequences and the wrong businesses being propped up. They are talking about the mass market producers like Renault, which recently received a share of a £6 billion hand-out from the French government. The BMW boss said, "If we go much further then there is a danger that we will have only one or two independent manufacturers and the rest will be state or semi-state owned. If governments did not get involved we would have a much stronger selection process, because then only companies with high liquidity and no cash-burn would survive. Both BMW and Mercedes are in this position... "

From Geneva comes word that one of Renault's most senior managers has said that the company wants F1 to cost less and demands a fairer share of the commercial revenues and that if this is not forthcoming "there really are no taboos" i.e. Renault would be quite prepared to quit.

This comes a day ahead of the FOTA press conference where these subjects will be addressed. FOTA is engaged in discussions with Bernie Ecclestone about the commercial revenues from 2013 onwards, not the short term.

* * *

The Formula One Teams Association was formed in September 2008 with all the teams signing up to it, including Ferrari. This was the first time they had all stood together and united against the FIA and Bernie Ecclestone to get a better deal financially and in governance terms. In March they faced the media and public for the first time. It represented a huge moment in the evolution of the sport and I had to be there.

* * *

FOTA cuts budgets by 50% and changes points
5 March 2009

The Formula One Teams Association held its first press conference today here in Geneva and the show of strength from the teams underlined how united they are.

The headlines are that they have agreed to measures for 2010 which will cut budgets by 50% compared to the 2008 season. This will mean teams like Force India needing a budget of around £50 million and a top team like Ferrari and McLaren operating on £150 million. It's impressive progress, but still some way short of what FIA president Max Mosley is looking for.

FOTA and Ferrari president Luca di Montezemolo told me afterwards that he thinks they will reduce costs still further in 2011 and 2012 but they are also looking to significantly increase revenues, particularly from the internet.

They have achieved the 50% saving for 2010 by making savings they are all comfortable with, such as a 50% cut in aerodynamics work, savings on gearboxes, a reduction in the number of updates allowed on the car in a season and a further cut in testing. They will also cut the cost of engine supply for small teams from £5 million per season to £3.2 million, so the complete engine and gearbox package will be under £5 million. They also agreed unanimously to standardise the KERS systems and a tender will go out shortly to that effect. (This is quite provocative and it will be very interesting to see what Max Mosley thinks of it...)

FOTA has also called for two significant changes to the racing for this season. Firstly they want races to be shortened to 150 miles from the current 200 and secondly for the winner to be better rewarded with a points system which goes 12-9-7-5-4-3-2-1. In addition the manufacturer teams will make gearboxes available to privateers for £1.5 million per season.

Montezemolo also confirmed that all the manufacturers in F1 have committed to stay in the sport until 2012, putting to bed any suggestion that Renault or Toyota might pull out and it was confirmed that the former Honda team will be on the grid in 2009.

Honda's Nick Fry was here and, although he would not give details, it seems a deal has been done to save that team. It is quite clear that without the FOTA initiatives of the last few months, the team would have been dead and buried and maybe one or two more teams would have followed.

All the teams will now sign the Concorde Agreement by 18 March and that will provide a lot of stability to the sport.

They have also agreed to provide more information for viewers this season to make the races more entertaining to watch, such as all the fuel data after qualifying, the radio conversations will be totally open and they want to make a graphic showing which cars are fuelled to the finish. Whether Bernie Ecclestone chooses to use these graphics on his TV feed is another question...

More on the background to Honda deal
6 March 2009

I'm delighted that Brawn GP has emerged from the rubble of the Honda GP team. It is a bold move by Ross and knowing him, he would not have done it if he did not think he could be successful. Everything he does he does well.

The money must be solid because Mercedes would not have done the engine supply deal if it wasn't. I understand that the money is coming from Honda.

Clearly it's an enormous challenge, but the rewards are potentially enormous for him too. After all he's now a major shareholder in a business with guaranteed income of at least £40 million per year (from TV) and on which Honda have spent £70 million in capital expenditure on hardware in recent years. If he keeps the team alive over the next few years and then, who knows, Honda comes back again, maybe as an engine supplier only, or if someone wealthy like a Mallya or Abramovich type wants to buy in, Ross will have a very valuable asset, which will make him very seriously rich.

Ross has said in the last few weeks that "my job is to save jobs" and although they will trim down the 700 workforce at Brackley, many of the jobs will be saved by this new team. We do not yet know whether there are any sponsors on the sidelines, but we do know that the deal would not have happened without FOTA teams supporting Ross and the new agreement for independents of three years engine and gearbox supply for under £5 million per season.

There is no truth in the rumours that Mike Gascoyne is the new technical director.

As for Mercedes, they are supplying the engine to the team and Brawn's engineers have had a Mercedes engine at Brackley since the end of January, to do the installation work. This means that they will have had less than two months to adapt their 2009 design to the Mercedes engine, which is very tight.

Ross will have seen this coming and will have put a working group in place to make the transition as smooth as possible. He is a consummate organiser and a genius at knowing exactly where to put human and technical resources and when.

Jenson Button and Rubens Barrichello will drive in this year's championship. Barrichello will extend his record as the most experienced driver ever and it's no surprise that Brawn chose him over Senna as he is a brilliant technical driver and he will help them far more than Senna would have done to get the car sorted quickly. Senna would have had a mountain to climb, learning F1 with no testing time.

It indicates that the finances must be solid because Senna brought around $10 million with him in sponsorship. Button has his severance pay from Honda so he will not be too out of pocket, whereas I imagine Rubens is on a lowish retainer, but he will just be happy still to be in F1.

* * *

A few days after the FOTA event I got on another plane and headed off to Barcelona for the last major test before the new season. All eyes were on the new Brawn-Mercedes car and right from the first morning of running it was quite clear to me that this car was a rocket ship. The last time I'd seen anything like it was the 1998 McLaren, which went on to win the drivers' and constructors' championships.

* * *

Get your money on Brawn for a Melbourne win!
13 March 2009

It's official! The Brawn is the fastest car in the F1 field with two weeks to go before the start of the season! It is an extraordinary story.

The Barcelona test, which finished on Thursday, could well go down as one of the most remarkable events in recent F1 history, as a team which seemed dead in the water at Christmas, bounced back and not only set the fastest outright lap of the week, but showed that it is faster over the race distance than the Ferrari!

Amazingly for a brand new car, reliability was very good too. The car covered over 2,000 kilometres during the four days using the same Mercedes engine (!) and there were very few technical issues.

It looks very much as though the battle for victory in Melbourne will be between Jenson Button and Rubens Barrichello, as long as the car lasts the distance. It has done two race distances in the last two days, so the omens are good. And the competition between the two Brawn drivers is fierce – yesterday Rubens was faster than Jenson was the day before over the long runs, but there was far less wind and the track was more rubbered in.

If you make a direct comparison between the race distance runs of Massa and Button on Wednesday and Barrichello on Thursday you see that Jenson does 19 laps below 1m 21, Barrichello does 14, while Massa manages just 2!

What is even more impressive is that on the 19th lap of his 20-lap first stint Rubens does a 1m 19.971 – startling proof that the Brawn looks after its tyres very well over a long run. The team really is in amazing shape! In contrast the Ferrari's lap times tail off into the 1m 22s at the end of the 20 lap stints.

In fact, so stunning was the Brawn's pace in Barcelona, it has caused all the F1 teams to revise completely their targets for the season. As I write this, there are briefings going on in all the team's factories as the full impact of the Barcelona data sinks in. Of course the teams will have big updates for Melbourne, which will make them faster, whereas the Brawn car is in Melbourne specification now, so the gap will close.

Also Brawn out front is not the best advertisement for KERS, as the team is not using it and won't be until later in the season, if at all.

Don't forget, Barcelona is a great yardstick for the season as it rewards aerodynamic efficiency and good tyre management, so if your car goes well there it's going to go well in most places.

One team engineer I spoke to remembers a meeting last season when the then Honda engineers said that they were going to be a long way ahead in 2009. Given where they were at the time, everyone laughed at this remark. They are not laughing now.

Jenson Button described his new car as "beautiful".

"It's been a stressful winter, five months out of the car," he said. "The plan B was not racing. But what would I do, sit at home? There's nothing out there for me. I'm 29 years old, I'm still a kid and I've still got a lot to prove. I'm here to try to win races with Brawn GP and I think there is a good possibility of that in the future."

It's early days yet, but it's been a great start to the adventure which is Brawn GP.

* * *

FOTA had been confident at its Geneva press conference that its proposals for cutting costs would be accepted by the FIA. But Max Mosley had other ideas. The FIA World Council voted through a hugely controversial rules package for 2010, whereby teams could run under a £30 million budget cap while those who didn't wish to, could spend what they liked, but would have more technical restrictions which would make their cars slower. It was provocative, inflammatory and it incensed FOTA. The war had begun...

* * *

Teams react badly to Mosley's £30m cost cap
17 March 2009

I nearly choked on my Rich Tea biscuit when the news came through about the £30 million budget cap and the two-tier system voted through today by the FIA World Motor Sport Council.

The teams, no doubt, did likewise. They did not expect this after presenting such a unanimous front the other week in Geneva. Their confidence that their unified voice would be heard by the FIA, when deciding rules and policy, was misplaced. Instead Max Mosley has gone much further than the teams wanted in stripping costs out of the sport. FOTA has just put a statement out which makes clear how annoyed they are with this move,

"With regard to the decisions taken today by the FIA World Council, FOTA would like to express its disappointment and concern at the fact that these have been taken in a unilateral manner," said FOTA president Luca di Montezemolo. "The framework of the regulations as defined by the FIA, to be applicable as from 2010, runs the risk of turning on its head the very essence of Formula 1 and the principles that make it one of the most popular and appealing sports.

"Given the timeframe and the way in which these modifications were decided upon, we feel it is necessary to study closely the new situation and to do everything, especially in these difficult times, to maintain a stable framework for the regulations without continuous upheaval, that can be perplexing and confusing for car manufacturers, teams, the public and sponsors."

The row has the potential to open up a dangerous rift between the Formula 1 teams and the FIA just as the new season starts. It is likely that Mosley has made this declaration/proposal to get teams to accept the general idea that there will be a budget cap system in F1, much as he did with standard Electronic Control Units, engine freezes and so on.

A £30 million budget cap will never be accepted, but once the teams have accepted the idea of a cap, Mosley probably reckons they will meet somewhere in the middle on the numbers, so around £50-60 million, which let's face it, should be enough to run an F1 team on. But the road ahead will be rocky and this is a real test of the mettle of FOTA as an organisation.

In Geneva I asked Montezemolo whether he thought Max would feel the FOTA proposals went far enough and he said that they would put them to him and have a dialogue. It's fairly clear that there hasn't been that much dialogue so far, not like in December when the FOTA engine package was quickly agreed by the FIA in the days following Honda's shock withdrawal.

What's behind this? Max wants to keep the smaller independent teams in the sport and encourage new ones to come in. He hates the idea that there are two empty franchises. But the budget cap puts manufacturer-backed teams like Ferrari, McLaren Mercedes and BMW in a difficult position.

Mosley proposes a two tier-system whereby manufacturers who do not want to run under a budget cap are to be given the option of spending as much as they like, but the budget capped teams will get more technical freedom, more engine power and better aerodynamics, to make them competitive. The boards of the big car firms will never accept this and you would have a two class F1, which never worked in the turbo/non-turbo days.

The eye-catching Mosley quote is the one where he dismisses suggestions that the budget cap would be impossible to police:

"We went into all this very carefully some time ago," he said. "We involved forensic accountants from Deloitte and Touche as well as financial experts from the current teams. The vast majority of payments are traceable and any benefits in kind can be valued. There were a number of meetings. It became clear we could do it."

The other little gem is this one: "We will make sure these advantages do no more than balance the disadvantages the cost-capped teams will have because of their very restricted budgets. As said, we will balance the median performances by adjusting the cost-capped cars should this prove necessary. The other cars will have stable technical regulations in return for which we understand FOTA intend to provide guarantees of continuing participation until 2012, underwritten by the major car manufacturers."

Mosley has leapt on the guarantee given in Geneva by the manufacturers to stay in until 2012 and thereby cut their wriggle-room on this. On top of that he's saying that the FIA may adjust the equivalence between capped and non-capped teams' performance, possibly even from race to race, which he knows is not really in the spirit of F1, but it's a strong position from which they will eventually have to agree something.

What makes this a particularly big play is the fact that these things have been voted through, so they aren't proposals, they are now rules which will need to be 'unmade' once any negotiations have taken place.

Expect more from FOTA on this.

Big names line up to attack new rules
19 March 2009

After the initial stunned silence over the decision to introduce a £30 million budget cap in F1, followed by a muted reaction from FOTA, today has seen some of the sport's biggest names express great unhappiness.

Chief among them is Ferrari and FOTA president Luca di Montezemolo, who didn't mince his words.

"It really is grave and absurd that our world finds itself in a situation like this. I hope for a climate of responsibility like that of the teams, who have reduced costs. It's really absurd and dangerous that one week from the first race F1 finds itself back in this kind of situation, which is very negative for credibility, for the teams, the manufacturers, the fans and sponsors.

"It's more important to have a calmer atmosphere and to avoid continual changes which generate uncertainty, for those who work in the sport, and raises question marks about the future."

That last bit is a veiled threat to take Ferrari out of F1, it seems to me. We'll hear more like that I think in the coming weeks.

Seven times world champion Michael Schumacher, who became close to FIA president Max Mosley through his work for the FIA Foundation, described the decision as "astonishing".

Renault team principal Flavio Briatore also came out and expressed his "shock" at the move:

"It was a bit of a shock," he said. "I believe all the parties need to be working together to achieve a target. The financial crisis makes everyone worried and we need Formula 1 to be more efficient but sometimes we are not happy with the sentences that are imposed.

"I believe the teams have already done an incredible job for 2009 and 2010, and now we're ready to go further but we need to continue working together with the Federation."

I still think that this is not a done deal, but rather a starting point, albeit a very firm one, in a negotiation with the teams over budgets in the short term and budget control in the long term. Think of it like the banking crisis. The governments loosened their regulation of banks and that led to banks taking bigger risks and doing things even they didn't understand, which has brought the world to the brink of a depression. What we will end up with as a result is a whole new system for regulating banks in the future.

In F1, teams have been allowed to spend what they want and the arrival of the manufacturer era in the sport around 2000 drove costs through the roof. No one was regulating that, the FIA accept that they should have done, and so we ended up with a model which is unsustainable in a recession. Drastic cuts were needed, the FOTA teams came up with what they thought was a pretty drastic package, but Mosley has gone much further and introduced an idea which will regulate budgets to make sure they don't get out of control in future.

At the same time, he's put the cat amongst the pigeons with FOTA, because the independent and smaller team owners will love the idea of a) making a profit and b) seeing the value of their franchise go through the roof, so they will want to back the plan. The manufacturer teams like Ferrari and McLaren have the most to lose from this and the unity of FOTA is put under strain.

A £30 million F1 team could only afford 25 employees, and so what you will probably see is more teams doing what Red Bull does and owning two teams. Mercedes will be looking at this, so too Ferrari. I wouldn't be surprised to see Jean Todt and his son popping up fairly soon with an F1 team and at least three of the GP2 teams could afford to go F1 racing on that basis.

There will now be a rush of new teams coming into F1, such as the US F1 outfit, and a waiting list will develop of wealthy people who want in. It will create a market.

Meanwhile Ross Brawn, who was given the Honda team plus a subsidy for year one, is sitting on an asset worth tens of millions of pounds.

Messy start to season in prospect
21 March 2009

It was all looking so good: Ross Brawn saves the Honda team, the car turns out to be a rocket ship, David threatens Goliath, a shake-up of the old order was in prospect. The racing was promising to be really close, with many teams on roughly the same pace. In other words a great season was in prospect, as many of you have said in your comments on this blog.

Yet now, with a week to go until the first race, we have the FIA backtracking on the winner-takes-all points rule, because the FOTA teams did not unanimously agree it; and then there is the virtual certainty of a messy technical protest into the legality of the diffusers on some of the cars, including Brawn, which will dominate the weekend and be well beyond the understanding of most of the fans and the media.

F1's capacity to shoot itself in the foot is to the fore again.

As I've been saying in my recent posts here since the Barcelona test, the Brawn car is seriously fast, perhaps fast enough to stay out front for quite a while before teams like Ferrari and BMW catch up. It would be intriguing if one of the Brawn drivers got a good head start on the field with four or five early wins. It would then be tough for another driver to get beyond that total. With McLaren seemingly out of the picture at the start of the season and the two Ferrari drivers likely to share any wins between them across the season, the way is clear if one of the Brawn guys can gain supremacy, to open up a bit of a lead, which under the winner-takes-all system might make him champion.

Ed Gorman writes in *The Times* that this is the suspicion of the FIA as to why the teams are now refusing to sign off on the new winner-takes-all system for deciding the champion.

Brawn's pace is certainly not going to encourage the other teams to sign up, but I think the real reason the teams have kicked back on this one is simply because they can. To bring in a new rule at short notice requires the teams to sign off on it unanimously and, stunned by the FIA's budget cap move, they've said, "You know what? We aren't going to do that, Max."

Mosley must have known that there was a risk of this and the blame appears to be being deflected on to the teams, but also on to Bernie Ecclestone, who allegedly told Mosley that the teams were on side with the new system. Maybe they were at the time, but given the opportunity to put the brakes on an FIA initiative, they've taken it.

In other words it's another step in what is now clearly going to be a drawn out battle between the FIA and the FOTA teams. It's not what anyone wants or needs, for a sport to appear not to know what the hell it's doing eight days before the start of a new season. One of my old heads of sport at ITV, a football man, used to say that he quite liked F1 as a spectacle, but that it too often opened itself up to ridicule. And that's what we have again here.

The FIA brought out some stunning material on Tuesday, particularly the £30 million budget cap, which would oblige the top teams to shed threequarters of their workforce, and would encourage a gold rush for new teams to come in to the sport.

FOTA's blocking move and the embarrassment caused to the FIA is likely to harden the FIA's resolve to leave the capped figure at £30 million, rather than negotiate it up to the £50-60 million which is more feasible.

* * *

Brawn's pace inevitably unsettled its rivals. One of the key technological innovations on the car was the so-called Double Diffuser, which gave the car a huge amount of downforce, and therefore grip, at the back of the car. Williams and Toyota also had a version of it on their cars but the other teams felt it was an illegal interpretation of the rules. There was a lot at stake because if the diffusers were ruled legal it would mean teams like McLaren and Ferrari being uncompetitive for at least the first half of the season.

* * *

Protest on Brawn imminent
25 March 2009

Just landed in Melbourne and I see that Red Bull has confirmed that it will protest the diffuser on the Brawn car, which it believes is worth half a second per lap.

Seven teams believe that the interpretations of Williams, Toyota and Brawn are outside the rules. It's one of those classic F1 moments you often get with a rule change, where someone spots a loophole, gets a performance advantage from it and the others cry foul. You can bet that if they had thought of it themselves they would have gone for it, because that's the nature of the beast.

The quotes are quite strong on this from Flavio Briatore. "It looks like there are two sets of regulations: the one that allows some teams to have the diffuser built in a certain way that is forbidden to others because it's considered illegal."

"It's illegal," agreed Red Bull's Helmut Marko. "We'll make a protest [Thursday] if the component isn't modified to conform to the regulations, because that diffuser guarantees a five-tenths [of a second] advantage per lap. Seven teams are certain it's illegal."

As I have said, Ross Brawn is a consummate organiser, and I imagine he has a plan B in case the diffuser is thrown out. How much that might damage their lap times will be interesting. I reckon they have a good second per lap in hand over the midfield and maybe six or seven-tenths over the Ferrari/BMW/Toyota battle.

FIA president Max Mosley gave an enigmatic response: "It's a very clever device and you can make a good case for saying it's legal and a very good case for saying that it's illegal."

So it's the stewards' call, here in Melbourne. As last year, they are headed by the FIA's Alan Donnelly.

Melbourne blog day 1
26 March 2009

I started the day collecting my F1 permanent pass; I can't believe this is my 20th season in the sport. As a TV person for the last 17 years, I always had a heavy, metal topped pass, issued by FOM. Now, although I am doing some work for Italy's RAI TV, because I represent the *Financial Times* newspaper, I fall under the FIA's jurisdiction and they have much smaller, lighter passes. I guess the TV people get the "bling" pass because they pay the big bucks to be here, tens of millions a year in rights fees, whereas newspapers are merely a necessary evil!

From the accreditation centre I travelled over by tram to the Westin Hotel in the city, where the Ferrari drivers did a Shell press briefing. Kimi was his usual eloquent self [not] while Felipe got quite worked up on a few issues. He hates the idea of the winner-takes-all points system. As a Ferrari driver you can see why. It's a system which calls for a team to have a clear number one and number two driver. He also described the U-turn last week over the points system as "a complete mess".

Meanwhile Kimi managed one smile, when a cameraman got up from his prone position in front of their table and knocked their glasses of water over. Kimi got a big rise out of that. Otherwise he was even more detached than he normally is. We'll see, but I felt from watching him in testing that he has rediscovered his sense of purpose. He's got his race face on again. I hope so, F1 needs a strong Kimi Raikkonen.

After Ferrari I jumped back on the tram and headed to the Stokehouse restaurant, on the St Kilda beach, to see the McLaren lot. They have been doing a lunch there for 11 years. Lewis Hamilton admitted that he was in new territory with a slow car, which has a lot of work in front of it to close the gap on the others. New team boss Martin Whitmarsh was on our table and looked very calm. In some ways they might wish they hadn't thrown so much effort at last year's car, as it seems to have cost them this year, but then again McLaren desperately needed to win that drivers' title after ten years of missing out.

Part of the McLaren event is a quiz, with some very obscure questions. A few people on my table knew the most obscure facts about F1 you could ever imagine. And guess what? We came away with a little trophy for winning the thing! Can't say I had much to do with it!

At the circuit, everything looked busy and colourful as usual. There is talk of the credit crunch, of teams laying people off, but the general mood is very positive, everyone excited to see where they are in the pecking order.

Behind the scenes most people are resigned to the fact that we are in for a long and painful battle between the FOTA teams, the FIA and Bernie Ecclestone. Some of the things that happen this weekend will be wrapped up in that political and financial struggle. But that's nothing new.

Three commanding presences
27 March 2009

An exhilarating hour spent in the pit lane during the first practice session. Strangely unfamiliar for me as it's three years since I was last down there, having had to yield my pit lane pass to my ITV colleague Steve Rider back in 2006. I used to live in the pits, knew every nook and cranny, had eyes in the back of my head for cars coming in, going out, mechanics rushing. It took me 20 minutes to get used to the rush and the energy again.

The energy is always astonishing; almost tangible. You can feel the drivers who have it, Massa is very aggressive straight away, Raikkonen looks intense and committed.

The Red Bull mechanics were already under pressure. Vettel had stopped out on the track early on and they were unscrewing the floor of Webber's car as I left the pit lane.

But what really caught my eye was three commanding presences in the pit garages.

At McLaren, Ron Dennis, dressed in black, stood on his own in the middle of the garage. The mechanics moved around him, respectfully, leaving a wide space around him. He looks very serious, has his aggressive face on. No longer the team principal maybe, no longer central to the activities on the pit wall, but still a huge presence in the garage.

Next door at Ferrari an equally serious-looking Michael Schumacher. An adversary of Dennis for many years, now a fringe player in a way, as a consultant to Ferrari, but they've built his part up a bit this weekend. With the switch to slick tyres and other new rules his eye and judgment are valued. He's taking the role seriously, moving across the garage to inspect Raikkonen's rear tyres when the car comes in from a run. He studies them, running his finger across the ruts and blisters. A young Bridgestone engineer, prodding his temperature gauge into the tyre, finds a stony-faced seven-time world champion grilling him about it. Schumacher, like Dennis, is a competitor. No longer directly competing, maybe, but still engaged, still totally committed.

Down the other end of the pit lane is the Brawn garage. The decoration is sparse, no frills, the cars sponsorless for the moment. If you didn't know better you'd think you were looking at the Minardi of today. But these guys are the team to beat this season. And the reason is Ross Brawn, Schumacher's old ally from Ferrari. His name is above the door, he's more committed than he's ever been and he's been smarter than everyone else in preparing for this year. Or should that be craftier? Actually it's both. Brawn cuts a massive figure on the pit wall, a radio on each hip, his face impassive.

Some work on the footwell of Button's car is taking longer than expected, Brawn comes off the pit wall to inspect it. The mechanics are aware of his presence and encouraged by it, but not intimidated by it. Unlike his old colleague Schumacher and his rival Dennis, Brawn is competing directly, he is right at the heart of what is happening.

All three of these huge characters, authors of much of the sport's recent history, were competing in their different ways on day one of a new Formula 1 season.

* * *

Not surprisingly the protest over the diffusers was thrown out by the Melbourne stewards. This left the protesting teams, who hadn't thought of the idea, in an awkward position...

* * *

Catch 22 for the teams who lost the protest
27 March 2009

A thought occurs to me. The seven teams who unsuccessfully protested about the diffusers of Brawn, Williams and Toyota are actually in a worse position than before. With the appeal not likely to be heard for at least a couple of weeks, what do they do now? Do they put their own copy of the Brawn diffuser in the wind tunnel and burn up valuable tunnel time which could be spent on something else, trying to make it work with their car, when the whole thing could be wasted if the appeal succeeds? Or do they forego that time in the tunnel with the copy but risk losing two weeks development time if the appeal finds for Brawn et al?

Very tricky. As a racer you'd go for option one. The other teams reckon it's worth half a second. They are having to catch up, and time is of the essence.

Behind the Virgin deal
28 March 2009

I followed curiously as Sir Richard Branson, accompanied by two dolly birds in Virgin t-shirts, made his way from the paddock gates to the Brawn GP garage to announce his sponsorship deal.

Branson knows a thing or two about getting publicity and this was an old-fashioned attention grab which worked a treat. He was answering questions from Sky TV Italy, flashbulbs popping all around him. At one point he turned to one of the girls and said, "I think we're doing rather well, don't you?"

The Brawn mechanics were still putting the stickers on the back-board for the press conference when the principals came out. It was all rather last-minute and very rock and roll.

John Button, Jenson's dad, was loving it all. He pointed to the Virgin logo on the wall, "Haven't seen one of those for ages," he quipped.

Branson said that he is investing heavily in "clean" fuels, which do not emit carbons. He said that he has a fuel ready for F1 and is going to try to persuade the car companies and F1 in general to use it. Shell, Mobil and Total, who invest heavily in Ferrari, McLaren and Renault, must have been interested to hear that.

The stickers on the car are quite small, indicating that this is a toe-in-the-water job. Branson said however that it is potentially a two stage deal. He's talking to us later in more detail and we'll find out if that means that he plans to take a shareholding in the team.

Brawn march on at the double
29 March 2009

I will never forget the feeling I had when I saw this Brawn car for the first time on the Monday morning in Barcelona on 9 March. It looked different, the detail on the car was so refined, and it went like stink.

Here was the most dominant F1 car we've seen since the Ferrari of 2004 and it was born out of the wreckage of the Honda team. Today they got a one-two finish in the first Grand Prix in Melbourne, making monkeys of the opposition in the process. How must Honda be feeling now? They pulled out of F1 just before Christmas, despite the assurances of Ross Brawn that the car would be a potential championship winner.

The executive who took that decision is like the man from Decca Records who turned down the Beatles. He would say it had to be done because car sales were plummeting, but the other manufacturers have stayed in and they didn't have a car like this one.

It's very likely that Brawn will dominate again in Malaysia, although the heat there will test the reliability of this car, which has still not done a huge mileage in testing. They have a good 8/10ths advantage over the Ferrari and more than a second over the McLaren. Both teams are frantically working on bringing new parts to the car at the next few races, hurling money at the problem, making a bit of a mockery of the concept of cost saving. For Ferrari to apply/utilise the diffuser properly requires a new gearbox casing, so it's a very big job. McLaren may have an astonishing manufacturing capability but they will need it because they are coming from a long way back.

As for Jenson Button, he appeared to be enjoying himself this weekend, always looked relaxed and happy, clearly not feeling pressure, revelling in the second chance that fate has given him. But behind the scenes he was very intense all weekend, apparently. He knows that this is his opportunity to do all the things he thought he was going to do in his career, before it went down the wrong path with Williams, then BAR and Honda.

I expect to see a more intense Button now, more single-minded, more ruthless even. He can take no prisoners from here, he has to translate this car advantage into results every time; if he can keep Rubens behind him nothing can stand in his way. If he can get far enough ahead in the points before the big teams wake up, he can win the world title. If they had stuck with the winner-takes-all model of deciding a championship, he'd have had an even better chance.

This Brawn car has been very carefully prepared and has come out of the oven perfectly cooked, whereas in comparison the grandee teams have whipped something up in the microwave. They now have to work hard to refine. It's unlikely that the FIA appeal court will help them by upholding their appeal against the Brawn diffuser so they are going to have to do it the hard way, in the wind-tunnel.

AUSTRALIAN GRAND PRIX
Melbourne 58 laps

1.	Button	Brawn GP		1h 34:15.784
2.	Barrichello	Brawn GP	+	0.807
3.	Trulli	Toyota	+	1.604
4.	Hamilton	McLaren-Mercedes	+	2.914
5.	Glock	Toyota	+	4.435
6.	Alonso	Renault	+	4.879
7.	Rosberg	Williams-Toyota	+	5.722
8.	Buemi	Toro Rosso-Ferrari	+	6.004

DRIVERS' STANDINGS
1. Button   10
2. Barrichello 8
3. Trulli   6
4. Hamilton   5
5. Glock   4
6. Alonso   3

CONSTRUCTORS' STANDINGS
1. Brawn GP   18
2. Toyota   10
3. McLaren-Mercedes   5
4. Renault   3
5. Williams-Toyota   2
6. Toro Rosso-Ferrari   1

Chapter Four
April 2009

After Melbourne I flew straight to Kuala Lumpur and went to a hotel on the coast along with some UK media colleagues. I had been puzzled by some contradictions between statements Lewis Hamilton had made to the media after the race and what was said after he saw the stewards. Late one night I got a tip-off that the FIA was looking into it. The post set traffic figures on the site soaring. It turned out to be a huge story and the repercussions for McLaren and Hamilton were immense. Not for the last time this season we had a situation where a young driver had been told by his team to cheat.

* * *

Hamilton could be in trouble in Malaysia
1 April 2009

A story has just appeared on the *Auto Motor und Sport* website in Germany, which could have explosive consequences for Lewis Hamilton and McLaren this weekend.

Written by Michael Schmidt, who is one of the most respected journalists in F1, the gist of the article is that Lewis Hamilton may have some explaining to do to the stewards about what he said to them in Melbourne, which led to him deposing Jarno Trulli from third place.

The story is headlined "Did Hamilton tell the truth?":

"Possibly the exclusion of Jarno Trulli in the season opener in Melbourne must be reopened. Doubts have emerged whether the beneficiary Lewis Hamilton told the truth to the hearing."

The story continues:

"The central issue however to be gleaned is whether the team instructed Hamilton to drive intentionally slowly. Hamilton answered in the negative. However after the race the following story circulated: Hamilton is said to have told a reporter that the team told him over the radio to let Trulli through again."

The story then develops:

"This contradiction brought the FIA officials to listen once again to the recordings of the radio traffic. Although there is no statement from official sources, speculation increases that the stewards from Melbourne will be reconvened in Malaysia."

It sounds like Lewis will either end up losing a point, or all of his points. If the stewards find that he misled them, he may face carrying a suspended ban over his head for a while, or worse...

* * *

Predictably it soon turned out that McLaren had misled the stewards and the team was obviously in a lot of trouble, this incident occurring barely 14 months after they were fined $100 million for misleading the FIA over their acquisition of Ferrari data. It was sad for me that Dave Ryan, the veteran McLaren team manager, lost his job over this weekend. Dave and I both serve on the Grand Prix Mechanics Charitable Trust board and have always got on very well. Dave is old school and there were rumours that the new management at McLaren had been looking for a way to move him on. But he was fully implicated in this story. His departure would be the first of several during this turbulent year as some of the veterans of the sport left under various clouds.

* * *

McLaren fall-out begins as Ryan is sent home
3 April 2009

The fallout from McLaren's Melbourne radio fiasco has begun with sporting director Dave Ryan suspended from duty and sent home from Malaysia. He is taking the rap for the heavy punishment the team and its driver Lewis Hamilton have received for misleading the stewards on an overtaking issue behind the safety car in Melbourne.

Team principal Martin Whitmarsh said: "In my 20-odd years working for McLaren, I doubt if I've met a more dedicated individual than Dave. He's been an integral part of McLaren since 1974 and has played a crucial role in the team's many world championship successes since that time.

"However, his role in the events of last Sunday, particularly his dealings with the FIA stewards, has caused serious repercussions for the team, for which we apologise. Therefore, I suspended him this morning and he has accepted this."

Ryan left the circuit mid-morning for the airport, apparently in tears, according to eye witnesses. He has been at McLaren since the 1970s, when he was a mechanic on James Hunt's 1976 world-title winning car. With the changeover of leadership from Ron Dennis to Martin Whitmarsh some of Dennis's oldest allies have left the team, including engineer Steve Hallam and Tyler Alexander. The team manager for many years, Ryan was given a promotion over the winter to sporting director and appeared to have a strong future at McLaren.

The team is in a process of change, with Dennis handing over the reins to Whitmarsh and beneath him Jonathan Neale. Ryan was a commanding presence at the team, a real disciplinarian. He will not be missed by some members of the team, to whom he gave a hard time, but his discipline might well be missed.

Whitmarsh will have to rally his team from this setback, albeit aware that there may well be more pain to come from the FIA World Council who will consider a disrepute charge. At the same time he will have some explaining to do to the Mercedes Benz board, who stuck with the team after the spy scandal of 2007, and who will be disappointed by this fresh blow to the team's image. Mercedes own just under 50% of the team with the rest of the shareholding split between the Bahraini royal family, Ron Dennis and Mansour Ojjeh.

Behind the scenes, Hamilton and his team will be having some frank exchanges. Only they know whether he was told to say what he said to the stewards or whether it was his own idea. Either way it has done damage to his sporting integrity.

Whitmarsh admits the team told Hamilton to lie
3 April 2009

A sensational press conference has just concluded here in Sepang, where new McLaren team principal Martin Whitmarsh admitted that his sporting director Dave Ryan deliberately set out to lie to the stewards in Melbourne and that he told Lewis to follow his lead. Whitmarsh suspended Ryan this morning and the New Zealander is on his way back to England as we speak.

Whitmarsh said that this matter did not go any higher in the McLaren organisation and that he was not consulted before Ryan and Hamilton went to the stewards.

"Lewis got out of the car and gave a truthful account of what happened (to reporters). When they got to the stewards, Dave, who had been part of what happened at Spa (Hamilton's penalty for passing Raikkonen by cutting a chicane in the Belgian Grand Prix last season, which many people felt was totally unfair) felt that the matter was highly sensitive and I think that in the heat of the moment his judgment was not to give a truthful account and I think Lewis was then led by that."

One of the things everyone wants to know is what was said in the original stewards' meeting, as we have only the FIA stewards' version of events as published yesterday. Whitmarsh said that he had not seen the transcript because one does not exist, "these things are not normally minuted and one of the stewards did not bring his notebook with him. All we can do is ask the driver and team manager what happened at the meeting."

Hamilton himself will speak soon here in Sepang. He has lied, that much is obvious, and as reigning world champion it puts a huge stain on his sporting integrity. He should have spoken to the media yesterday having first sorted out the details with Ryan and Whitmarsh, but instead, the whole thing has been allowed to ramp up and in the absence of Hamilton's side of the story, his reputation has taken a hammering. He now has to admit, "I lied, I was told to and I'm sorry," after the event.

I hate to keep comparing this to moments in Michael Schumacher's career, but in 1994-95 he felt that he had to move away from Benetton because of all the allegations of cheating, from the FIA, which were piling up against the team and reflecting badly on him. So he moved to Ferrari in 1996.

Steadying the ship generally will be Whitmarsh's first priority, but after that he will have to work hard to persuade Hamilton that staying with the team is his best long-term option.

A bit of light relief from Vettel
3 April 2009

In an intensely feverish atmosphere here in Sepang, as the situation around McLaren and Lewis Hamilton intensifies and threatens to spiral out of McLaren's control, a bit of light relief has been offered by Sebastien Vettel.

The German driver says in the Red Bull press release reviewing today's track action:

"It's very hot and no matter how much you prepare, the first outing is a bad surprise. Fortunately I've got a bag with dry ice in it, which I put next to my balls, so at least they stay nice and cool."

Two questions, Seb:

1. What happens if you have a shunt and the bag bursts?
2. Does this reveal which part of your anatomy really does the thinking?

Hamilton makes sure the world knows he's sorry
3 April 2009

Things are moving so fast here in Sepang it makes your head spin. Lewis Hamilton has just made an appearance in the media centre and given what has to be the most frank and open admission of guilt and regret we have seen in this sport.

He sat alone on the stage and spoke for a little over ten minutes, his voice cracking at times, his body language full of anguish and regret.

"I went into the meeting wanting to tell the story and I was misled. I was instructed and misled by my team manager to withhold information and that's what I did. I sincerely apologise to the stewards for wasting their time. I'm very sorry for the situation. Sorry to all my fans, who have believed in me. Who I've showed you I am the past three years is who I am; I'm not a liar, I'm not a dishonest person, I'm a team player and every time I've been informed to do something I've done it. This time I realise it's a huge mistake and I'm learning from it. It's taken a huge toll on me.

"This is the worst thing I've experienced in my life and that's why I'm here, because it's right for me as a human being and as a man to stand up here in front of you all and tell you exactly what went on and say how sorry I am. I'm sorry to the team, to my family for the embarrassment.

"I'm sure that the FIA will act accordingly and in the right way."

He added that Trulli had driven a great race and that "it wasn't my intention to get him a penalty."

By making such a frank admission, it's likely that Hamilton will escape a ban, even a suspended one. The damage to his reputation and the loss of the result in Australia are likely to be deemed punishment enough.

Hamilton and Ryan have been in the stewards' room together on many occasions over the past two years and the only thing we didn't get the chance to ask is whether this is the first time Ryan "instructed" Hamilton to lie. I'm sure that the FIA will consider this when the World Council look at the situation.

Hamilton has been criticised in the past for not putting his hands up and saying "sorry" often enough. He couldn't avoid it on this occasion.

One thing he will have to deal with is the impression many of his critics have that he is a manufactured driver, not his own man. The fact that he went along with the deception, didn't take a stand at the time, even though he knew what he was doing was wrong, will reinforce that impression.

The room was full of media from all around the world, with the Fleet Street boys on the front row. At the end there was a light round of applause from some journalists, as Hamilton walked from the room, his shoulders sagging.

How the public will view him now, only time will tell, but it's been a savagely bad start to the season for him, for McLaren and for new team principal Martin Whitmarsh. Other teams are surprised that McLaren has allowed this to come down to individuals, that they have not stuck together as a team. By singling out Ryan, they have acted in a way that is different from the team spirit of McLaren in the past.

Why Button's Malaysia win today was masterful
5 April 2009

It's a shame that Jenson Button has yet to see the chequered flag at full racing speed at the end of a full race. Both his wins have been terrific, but this one today was really special and you have to pay tribute to the masterful way that the Brawn team, Button and his engineer Andrew Shovlin managed the changing conditions.

Others, like Glock and Heidfeld, made greater gains by gambling on wet tyres, and Heidfeld gambled several times with the result that he made only one pit stop compared to Button's four. But then Glock and Heidfeld had nothing to lose, while Button had everything.

He said afterwards that the car wasn't very well balanced on wet tyres, so it was a credit to him that he was able to keep his pace up in the wet conditions.

"The conditions we had today, it's very unusual to drive the full wets in slightly greasy conditions, we had to go for that option because we thought it was going to rain and we were in the lead. It felt pretty terrible, the rear was always trying to break away. But that was more down to the conditions.

"When we put the intermediates on, the car felt pretty good. I had a good balance for the car, because it was the right tyre for those conditions, until it started bucketing it down and then no tyre was usable."

So he did his bit. But the team did a brilliant job. If you compare his outcome with Nico Rosberg's you'll see what I mean, Rosberg had the

MALAYSIAN GRAND PRIX
Sepang 56 laps

1. Button	Brawn GP	55:30.622
2. Heidfeld	BMW Sauber	+ 22.722
3. Glock	Toyota	+ 23.513
4. Trulli	Toyota	+ 46.173
5. Barrichello	Brawn GP	+ 47.360
6. Webber	Red Bull-Renault	+ 52.333
7. Hamilton	McLaren-Mercedes	+ 60.733
8. Rosberg	Williams-Toyota	+ 71.576

DRIVERS' STANDINGS

1. Button	15
2. Barrichello	10
3. Trulli	8.5
4. Glock	8
5. Heidfeld	4
6. Alonso	4

CONSTRUCTORS' STANDINGS

1. Brawn GP	25
2. Toyota	16.5
3. BMW-Sauber	4
4. Renault	4
5. Williams-Toyota	3.5
6. Toro Rosso-Ferrari	3

early lead and was on a similar strategy to Button, just a couple of laps shorter on the first stop. He had the pace for a podium today. And yet he made stops on laps 27 and 30 and slipped from 2nd to 8th, with the fourth stop from inters to wets, a stop other cars didn't make. This could have happened to Button, but he kept the momentum going and at every stage the team stayed calm and did what was required.

Today's other great revelation is that we got to see just how fast this Brawn car really is, when Jenson had to push hard in his two laps before his first stop, in order to leapfrog Rosberg and Trulli. He did a 1m 36.641, which was a second faster than the next non-Brawn car!

That is quite some margin they have, greater than we had imagined previously and it's also impressive to note that that lap time was set at the end of a 16 lap stint on soft tyres, so the Brawn can be said to have fantastic tyre management ability.

Ferrari start to get worried
5 April 2009

Two races in and still no points on the board for Ferrari. Of course they can point to the effort put in to win last year's title and to the row over the two-step diffusers which Brawn, Toyota and Williams have, but the fact of the matter is that both of these races have offered opportunities for Ferrari and McLaren to score points but they haven't taken those chances.

In two normal dry races, maybe the "diffuser three" would have had an advantage, but these last two races have given the non-diffuser teams opportunities - in Melbourne the two safety cars levelled the playing field, in Sepang it was the rain.

But what will worry team boss Stefano Domenicali the most is the decision-making process has been poor.

In qualifying the track was ramping up very quickly; I tweeted on it from early in the session, it was as plain as the whatnots on a dog and yet they thought Massa would be safe on a modest lap and he was caught out. Today the decision to switch Kimi onto full wet tyres when the track was bone dry at the time was totally insane.

Reliability has been a concern too for Ferrari; Raikkonen had another KERS-related problem this afternoon, on top of the issues in Australia.

Domenicali had a hard edge to his voice when he spoke this evening in Sepang. "It's not a positive weekend, the second in a row and this is not good at all. We have to react immediately. People have to take responsibility for things, from a performance point of view and from a management point of view. This is not acceptable and I do not accept it."

As for who decided to put Kimi on wet tyres on a dry track, Domenicali commented, "I don't want to say, because we need to discuss it internally. But I can tell you why we did it, which is that we knew a big storm was coming and we felt a few spots of rain, so because of this, one plus one, that was the decision."

The rain came 6 minutes later...

Ferrari president Luca di Montezemolo had been on the phone to poor Stefano. "He is not happy, this is normal in his position, I'm not happy either."

So where do they go from here?

"From a performance point of view, we need to make sure that we can bring something to China. On the aero side we know what we need to make the difference. We need more downforce. We also need to see why on Friday our car on soft tyres with lots of fuel was very competitive, but with other tyres was very difficult. So the car is very sensitive to fuel load and tyres. On the management side we need to improve because this is something we cannot accept for the future."

Meanwhile a totally hacked-off Kimi Raikkonen, was even more mono-syllabic than usual. His assessment of the first two races: "In the first race I made a mistake so we lost some points, here we made completely the wrong tyre choices."

It's still only early days and Ferrari had some blank weekends the last two years and still won championships. But they have to get on the scoreboard in China and hope that Jenson Button hits trouble, otherwise he could be 20 or 30 points clear by the time we get back to Europe next month.

* * *

Shortly after the event Ferrari wielded the axe; the senior management was restructured and Luca Baldisserri, who had taken over the race team track operations and strategic part of Ross Brawn's role when Ross left the team at the end of 2006, lost that responsibility to Chris Dyer, formerly Michael Schumacher's race engineer.

* * *

Fresh insight into McLaren case
10 April 2009

I'm grateful to one of my readers, doctorvee, for posting a very interesting comment here on the *JA on F1* site. He highlights an interview which McLaren boss Martin Whitmarsh gave to the BBC at the end of the Australian Grand Prix.

"...there's some debate about whether it's a 3rd place at the moment given that Trulli fell off and re-passed under the Safety Car..."

[Ted Kravitz asks him to expand on this.]

"...At the end, under the Safety Car, Trulli fell off on to the grass and Lewis had no choice but to go past him. He was not on the racing circuit. Trulli then re-took the place under the Safety Car, which ordinarily you wouldn't do. I know that the FIA are looking at it at the moment and doubtless we'll have a ruling in due course."

doctorvee adds: "Martin Whitmarsh was not asked if there were any radio conversations. But he chose to omit this information regardless. The BBC's viewers were left with the impression that Jarno Trulli had passed Lewis Hamilton of his own accord, not that he had been invited to do so. This version of events is very similar to the one we are led to understand was relayed to the stewards.

"This would seem to suggest that very soon after the end of the race, a version of events - the official McLaren party line, as it were - was constructed. This is the version of events that Martin Whitmarsh gave to Ted Kravitz and the BBC's viewers. "

His conclusion from all this is that the line presented by Davy Ryan in the stewards' room was the team's party line, not the act of a "rogue employee", as it is now being presented. The significance of this is that the FIA WMSC will seek to analyse the degree to which others in the team were involved.

Whitmarsh shows that he is eager to secure the third place. But the word "ordinarily" is the one that catches my eye here, as it shows that a degree of reflection is taking place, but also that there may be extenuating circumstances. It almost invites a sub-clause in brackets, such as ...(unless invited to do so...)

Meanwhile the FIA has released some more information on the second stewards' hearing in Sepang, which appears to show Hamilton and Ryan sticking to their line that Trulli passed without invitation, despite being played recordings of both the original radio traffic and Hamilton's post-race interview, where it is quite clear he had understood that the team was telling him to let Trulli through.

*   *   *

The above post played a part in what happened next in the McLaren saga. The FIA read it, picked up on the anomaly in the McLaren story and requested the interview tapes from the BBC, which were presented as evidence at the hearing.

*   *   *

Diffusers legal but it got very personal
15 April 2009

The International Appeal Court has ruled that the diffusers used by Brawn, Toyota and Williams are legal. So now we have clarity and we move on, although there will be rumblings from the other teams. They can do nothing more though and have to bring their own versions of the double-decker to their cars as quickly as possible.

This decision could well decide the outcome of the world championship in Brawn's favour: certainly that is the view of former world champions Fernando Alonso and Kimi Raikkonen, who are on the wrong side of the debate. Ferrari, McLaren, Renault and Red Bull know that the first four races - a quarter of the season - have been lost with the decision going against them. Brawn and its drivers Jenson Button and Rubens Barrichello have a very healthy head start and should dominate at least the next couple of races before the others are able to fit their own double diffusers and close the performance gap.

Bad feelings remain over this issue. The hearing yesterday certainly got nasty, it seems, as it dragged out into yesterday evening, Paris time.

It was a bruising encounter for the protagonists, with some real niggle between former colleagues and lawyers getting stuck in to others' reputations. But some of the things said yesterday will surely come back to haunt those who said them.

The impression the protesters are keen to give is that they are unanimous in their feeling that the three diffuser teams have not only been crafty, but have violated the spirit of sporting competition.

Certainly I'm told that all the teams are backing the protest, with the exception of Toro Rosso (no point in the owner paying twice if his other team, Red Bull, have already paid) and Force India, for political reasons.

One argument, advanced by Adrian Newey and Flavio Briatore, is that the diffusers should be banned on safety grounds, on the Brawn car in particular, because they make the cars too fast.

Although three teams are in the dock, only one team owner seems to be getting the flak and that is Ross Brawn. He had to sit there, while Nigel Tozzi, Ferrari's lawyer and a man who was on the same side as Brawn until two years ago, described him as a "person of supreme arrogance", because he sees things one way when everyone else sees things a different way. "Only a person of supreme arrogance would think he is right when so many of his esteemed colleagues would disagree," he roared.

Instead, Brawn is now looking like a person of supreme intelligence.

Tozzi then went on to say something that a lawyer representing an F1 team in an FIA hearing really should have thought twice about saying, because the words will surely be used against him one day: "Anyone with a command of English will tell you it is a (loop)hole, so do not let someone attempting to be clever with words defeat the express purpose of the rules."

Being clever with words to defeat the purpose of the rules is what getting an edge in F1 is all about. It happens every time someone comes up with something the others haven't got and every time there is a protest and an appeal into some genius device, or loophole.

Ferrari have been known to benefit from such a situation themselves. I remember in 1999 sitting in a steaming hot Ferrari office in Sepang after the race as Ross Brawn showed us with a ruler why the barge-boards had been ruled illegal by the stewards. And yet a few days later, through using clever words at a hearing in Paris, Ferrari's lawyer managed to get the judges to agree that by viewing the car from a certain angle and by applying tolerances mentioned elsewhere in the rules, the barge-boards were legal after all.

Brawn may forgive and forget, maybe not. But I was very surprised to hear Tozzi having a go at the FIA for inconsistency. The FIA denies that other teams had applied to use a similar diffuser design and were knocked back. In any case I was surprised to see Tozzi using the terms he used: "The position of the FIA is totally baffling. We urge you to save the FIA from itself," he is alleged to have said, according to the Press Association.

That is strong stuff. Whatever you may think of the historical relation-ship between Ferrari and the FIA, this line shows you that as of right now, they are at loggerheads and that there is a huge amount of frustration on Ferrari's side with the FIA's position on this issue, with the way they have allowed this dispute to develop. The FIA say that their position is clear and has always been consistent: the diffusers are legal.

Also bear in mind that Ferrari president Luca di Montezemolo heads the team's association, FOTA, and is more than a little discouraged by the way the FIA World Council ignored all of FOTA's hard work and suggestions and instead voted in the £30 million budget cap for 2010.

These things work themselves through in the end and Ferrari and the FIA will be friends again at some point in the future.

Dennis falls on his sword, but what will be the effect?
16 April 2009

Ron Dennis announced today that he is stepping down as CEO and chairman of McLaren Group and has walked away from all racing activities, a decision he says is unconnected with the team's current disciplinary problems and which he reached alone.

He handed over the team principal role to Martin Whitmarsh at the start of the season, but was still a forceful presence in the team and a shareholder. It appears that he will still have that shareholding, but has agreed not to attend races and to distance himself from the team.

Dennis has a plan B, which is that he will head McLaren Automotive, making road cars, a business which later this year will be spun off from the McLaren Group. He has said that he wants to double the company's value in the next five years. The new chairman of McLaren is Richard Lapthorne, the current chairman of Cable and Wireless Plc. Dennis and Whitmarsh will both report to him.

It is often said that all political careers ultimately end in disappointment and the same is often true of other competitive animals, like sports figures and particularly racers. Dennis has had a stunningly successful career thanks to his relentless attention to detail and determination, but in the last few years he has repeatedly left himself and his organisation exposed, as they are now over the lying scandal in Melbourne. Partnerships like those with Mercedes and key sponsors are at stake.

A career like Dennis's should have ended with a final world championship followed by a knighthood, but the spy scandal of 2007 can't have helped that cause and any association with what went on in Melbourne would add to the damage. To quit now appears to be a sign that this mighty career is ending in disappointment.

There has been widespread speculation about the timing and motive for this move. Dennis has categorically denied that it has anything to do with the Melbourne "liargate" scandal and the FIA hearing on 29 April. It is being presented as Ron's own work, not the result of a back-room deal with Max Mosley, nor of a power play by Anthony Hamilton.

It is quite plausible that he thinks that by stepping away from the team now, drawing the sting, if you will, that the team will escape the kind of punishment which might cause its very existence to come into question, such as exclusion from the rest of the 2009 season. I still don't believe that this will happen, but if it did, it would rupture the relationship with many of the sponsors and would test the resolve of shareholder Mercedes, which has a 40% stake..

Some commentators see the hand of Lewis's father, Anthony Hamilton, in this departure. It is no secret that he spoke several times to Max Mosley over the course of the Malaysian GP weekend and his anger at the way the team allowed the situation to unfold around, and damage, his son was clear. I'm fairly sure he put pressure on the team to agree for Whitmarsh to issue the full apology in that Friday press conference in Sepang and he was instrumental in briefing Lewis as to what to say in his own press meeting shortly afterwards.

But would he have had the clout to force Dennis to step down from the team in which he still retains a 15% shareholding? Did Anthony remove the man who had nurtured Lewis since he was 13 years old and gave him his opportunity in F1?

As world champion and F1's biggest box office draw, Lewis Hamilton has significant power, but I can't see that it is sufficient on its own to bring about a move like this.

Myself, I think this is a tactical play. Dennis knew in 2007 that if he fell on his sword and walked away the spy scandal would have had a less painful ending, but he chose not to do that. Perhaps his reading of the situation now is that this is the only way to avoid obliteration for the team. If so, it rather suggests that he believes his role will be uncovered on 29 April and he's positioning himself and the team for that.

* * *

McLaren boss Martin Whitmarsh wrote to the FIA before the hearing admitting to all of the charges against them. He took the pragmatic approach which Dennis refused to do in 2007. Coupled with Dennis's departure the letter had the desired effect. At the World Motorsport Council hearing on 29 April McLaren was given a three-race ban, suspended for 12 months.

* * *

Briatore goes for it... big time!
17 April 2009

A furious Flavio Briatore continues to rage about the unfairness of Formula 1.

After some savage comments in Melbourne about the integrity of Ross

Brawn, his former technical director, the Renault boss has now laid into the FIA and the drivers currently at the front of the field. He claims that a pecking order of Brawn, Williams and Toyota shows that F1 has lost all its credibility,

"The drivers in our teams are all world champions and instead there's a driver who's a semi-pensioner and another, a decent bloke, but he's a kerbstone, fighting for the world championship. (A reference to Barrichello and Button respectively.) I don't know how we can say we have credibility."

"It's impossible to make up the ground to those teams. In three or four races the championship will be decided and I can't see the interest for spectators to watch a Grand Prix, when Button has 60 points and Nakajima has 50. Better to listen to the radio or go and do something else."

Briatore has won four world championships, two with Schumacher in the Benetton days and two with Alonso in the Renault days. In none of those seasons did his team have the kind of advantage that Brawn now enjoys; it was always a very tight battle for him with Williams, McLaren and Ferrari. Although the mass damper on Alonso's Renault, before it was banned, gave Renault something the others didn't have, it did not put them well clear of the opposition, as Brawn is today.

Briatore's outbursts have confused some of his fellow team principals. He is part of FOTA, indeed he heads the commercial working group, and yet in recent weeks his outbursts against other teams have made it look as though the spirit of FOTA unity now lies in shreds. He is a close friend of Bernie Ecclestone, and the pair are usually seen together most evenings at Grands Prix. Asked about Briatore's comments, Ecclestone said, "Everyone is entitled to their opinion."

Flavio also sets his sights on the FIA for allowing a situation to develop which goes completely against the notion of cost saving.

"At a time when we are talking about bringing down budgets to £30 million a year, we have spent £15m on KERS and another £10 million on diffusers. So that leaves five more for travel and paying the employees!"

And in the background is another agenda; that of FOTA and what it might do next and what Briatore's part in it might be, if F1 proceeds down the path it is currently on with budget caps and other radical rule changes for 2010.

Vettel flawless as Red Bull take 1-2 finish in China
19 April 2009

Renault boss Flavio Briatore said this weekend that the current pecking order undermines F1's credibility. But today's was a great race with stellar performances at the front from Sebastian Vettel and Mark Webber, who scored a Red Bull one-two, the team's first F1 victory. Jenson Button and team-mate Rubens Barrichello were struggling to get the wet tyres to work as well as on the Red Bull but managed third and fourth places.

Meanwhile the grandee teams, whom Briatore believes should be at the front, Ferrari, McLaren and Renault, all had another difficult day. Ferrari got no points again for the third race, while Renault turned second place on the grid into ninth at the finish. McLaren fared a little better with fifth and six places.

Briatore's credibility point was related to the diffuser situation but not only do Red Bull not have a double diffuser, today the rain was a great leveller and still the grandees didn't take advantage.

This was Vettel's second ever win, again in the wet just as last year in Monza. "Every lap there was a lot of aquaplaning," said the German. "We knew we had to push to get away from the pack. I had the best conditions because I had no car in front of me for most of the race. I'm extremely happy, the second time in wet I've won. The car was fantastic. We were struggling with reliability yesterday but the team fixed it and we got a 1-2 for Red Bull."

Vettel took the blame for a curious incident when Sebastien Buemi collided with him during the safety car period; he had backed off because he thought Trulli's slow-moving car in front was Barrichello and didn't realise that Buemi was behind him.

CHINESE GRAND PRIX

Shanghai 56 laps

1. Vettel	Red Bull-Renault	1h57:43.485
2. Webber	Red Bull-Renault	+ 10.970
3. Button	Brawn GP-Mercedes	+ 44.975
4. Barrichello	Brawn GP-Mercedes	+ 1:03.704
5. Kovalainen	McLaren-Mercedes	+ 1:05.102
6. Hamilton	McLaren-Mercedes	+ 1:11.866
7. Glock	Toyota	+ 1:14.476
8. Buemi	Toro Rosso-Ferrari	+ 1:16.439

DRIVERS' STANDINGS

1. Button	21
2. Barrichello	15
3. Glock	10
4. Vettel	10
5. Webber	9.5
6. Trulli	8.5

CONSTRUCTORS' STANDINGS

1. Brawn GP-Mercedes	36
2. Red Bull-Renault	19.5
3. Toyota	18.5
4. McLaren-Mercedes	8
5. Renault	4
6. Toro Rosso-Ferrari	4

Mark Webber observed after the race that when the wet tyres lose their edges they don't cut through the water as well and that was a factor for many drivers.

Jenson Button was philosophical about not being able to match the Red Bull cars. "Everyone was struggling with aquaplaning," he said. "The last corner was a lake. It was a struggle with tyres shuddering, I couldn't get temperature into the tyres. I don't know why - obviously our car works in a different way. I couldn't challenge Red Bull, they were immensely quick."

Meanwhile Lewis Hamilton, who has historically excelled in the wet, started very confidently, making a lot of moves and passes. But he got into a vicious spiral as his wet tyres wore down because he was on a one-stop strategy and asked too much of them. Lewis had a series of spins. Team-mate Heikki Kovalainen got ahead of him towards the end of the race.

Button extended his championship lead and now must be looking at Vettel as his main rival apart from his own team-mate. The big names are a long way behind, with only Hamilton getting any kind of score on the board with a sixth of the season already gone.

So is Red Bull now a top team?
19 April 2009

Form is temporary, class is permanent. That is the great adage of the sporting world. So what are we to make of what's happening at the moment in F1? Is this the start of a change of order, with great names like McLaren, Renault and Ferrari in decline and emerging teams like Red Bull and Brawn the new top dogs?

Anyone who says that would be guilty of serious short-term thinking. Those three teams deserve great respect for their record of success spanning many years, and they are not to be written off so easily.

If you look at the first three races of the season, with two wins for Brawn and one for Red Bull and glance across at the constructors' championship, where those two teams top the table with McLaren a distant fourth, Renault creeping along in sixth and Ferrari yet to get off the mark, you may say to yourself, "double diffusers". Except that you remember that Red Bull doesn't have one of those, so then you might say to yourself, "Ah well, the top teams were pushing right to the end of last season, whereas Brawn and Red Bull were on 2009 by then." And you would have a point.

But does this mean that the old order will be returned once the top teams get their clever aero parts? Can Brawn and Red Bull stay out front all season and if they do, will they be able to do it again next year?

In my live twitter feed of today's race, one of my final postings suggested that Sebastian Vettel has now done enough to show the "top teams" what he has to offer and to speculate how long Red Bull would be able to hold on to him.

Then you contemplate the main item on the agenda when FOTA next meets the FIA; the budget cap. This is like the time bomb, which was planted in F1 a few weeks ago and has since been forgotten in all the hype about the McLaren liargate scandal and the three crazy races we've been enjoying.

Not many people in F1 believe that the budget cap will happen as billed, but it's looking like a budget restriction of some kind will come in and that will limit the ways in which the old "top teams" can beat the new "top teams".

Brawn is a good example of a team which, as Honda, was guilty of the spending excesses of all the F1 manufacturers. Now with a smaller staff, a leaner budget and a customer engine, it is a shining example of the formula that the older teams must emulate if they are to limbo under the budget cap bar next season. It's been painful for the staff who have been laid off, but it's given Max Mosley an example to point at and say, "That's what I'm talking about."

Red Bull is built on the same model... a pattern is starting to emerge here. If we think like Darwin about this, the survival of the fittest and the most fitting and all that, then the teams at the front now are already equipped for the evolution F1 is to undergo in 2010. Of course the weakness is that those customer engines have to come from manufacturers and that could all get quite political.

This season is far from over and I'm sure we all expect Ferrari, Renault and McLaren to win before the final race. And we find it hard to imagine that they won't be back fighting for the title in 2010. But they have a lot on their collective plate at the moment and if the financial playing field is levelled next year, we could end up with a lot of "top teams".

So maybe Vettel will stay put after all...

Briatore gives Piquet one last chance
24 April 2009

Flavio Briatore has spoken in support of his driver Nelson Piquet, who has endured another disappointing start to the season in the Renault. At the last race in Shanghai, Piquet was half a second slower in qualifying than his team-mate, Fernando Alonso. But Alonso had the only example of Renault's new double diffuser. Here this weekend the team has new parts on both cars, including modifications to the front wing and front suspension.

The pressure is really on Piquet in qualifying tomorrow. Judging from today's running the Renault is capable of getting both drivers into the top ten, with Alonso targeting fifth or sixth place. Any repeat of the last two qualifyings where Piquet was eliminated in the first run will increase the pressure on the driver.

Briatore has in the past not spared his drivers' blushes, but he seems to be going out of his way to give Piquet every possible chance to make a go of his opportunity. Piquet's father raced with Briatore in the Benetton in the early 1990s and the two have been close ever since.

Last year Piquet started badly but improved his form as the year went on, boosted by a second place finish in Germany and a very strong drive in Japan to end the season.

Briatore has gone out on a limb to protect Piquet Junior, but time is running out and Piquet probably has at best a handful of races to save his seat. Briatore elegantly and somewhat obliquely admitted as much this afternoon:

"You see the performance as well. Everyone is watching TV, including me and it's what you see, " he said. "It's a difficult moment for him. In a moment like this you don't need to kill anybody you need to support and to hope, hope he'll do better. This is his first race with a normal situation [he has a double diffuser, like Alonso] and let's see. Sunday or Monday hopefully we will have a different idea. "

Piquet seems to be vulnerable to pressure and to need a long time to get up to speed and a lot of practice to be able to perform. He's not terribly adaptable and F1 demands that quality from its top drivers. With little testing before the season started and none between races,

Piquet appears to be struggling to have confidence in his car. If he is moved out, it is likely GP2 driver Romain Grosjean will be promoted.

Button clears the air with third win from four races
26 April 2009

Jenson Button and the Brawn team took their third win in four races this afternoon at the Bahrain Grand Prix, ahead of Sebastian Vettel, but the result could have gone either way. The two cars were very evenly matched. What made the difference was that Button was bold at the start and thereafter was able to run in clear air and Vettel wasn't.

The key moment of the race came at the end of the first lap, when Button was able to pass Lewis Hamilton under braking into turn one. This allowed him to run in clear air ahead of Hamilton, while Vettel was held up by the McLaren driver, losing ten seconds in the first 15 laps.

Vettel's strategy was for him to run four laps longer than his main rivals, but he was not able to exploit this because he was held up. Consequently he wasn't able to build enough of a margin over Trulli in the four laps he had in clear air and when he rejoined after his pit stop he found himself behind Trulli.

To make matters worse, Trulli's Toyota team had made a mistake on tyre choice and Trulli was on the hard tyre, which was a second per lap slower than the soft. So Vettel lost another ten seconds and with them his chance to fight Button for the win.

Neverthless, it was another strong result for Vettel and Red Bull. The young German said afterwards that he hopes and expects to be able to challenge Button more closely in the next few races when he gets some more updates.

Button had some reliability concerns today. The team cut some holes in the bodywork to help the cooling and at times Button turned the engine down from maximum revs to protect it. He admitted afterwards that if he had had Vettel's race, following other cars for most of the time, the car would have overheated and he would have had to drop back.

Three wins and a third place from the first four races is an impressive haul. Button now has 31 points but it would have been 36 if the Malaysian race had gone the full distance and been awarded full points.

It looks as if Vettel and Red Bull will be challenging him for the title and I think Hamilton and McLaren will too. Their rate of development has been stunning and they have the double diffuser to come in Spain or Monaco.

Brawn have really capitalised on their performance advantage at the start of the season and even squeezed a win out here where they did not really have the fastest car, either in race or qualifying trim. Toyota had the fastest lap in both, but Brawn was able to carve the win out of the opportunity Button gave them by passing Hamilton early on (the McLaren having eased past him at the start using the KERS button).

Button said after the race that he had no idea what the state of play would be when the teams reconvene in Barcelona, given that most people will have virtually new cars.

"We've got an upgrade (believed to be worth three-tenths of a second per lap) coming in Barcelona. I just hope that it's enough. Nobody knows. And the thing is that we can't go testing either, so we don't get that chance to get the feel for it."

This Brawn car is the result of over a year's development, representing an enormous investment from Honda, and exploits a clever loophole in the rules that others are now free to copy. From here on it's about keeping the developments coming. The team may not have the resources of the leading teams to spend on development, but it does have a year's head start.

ITV F1 wins third straight BAFTA for Brazil GP coverage 26 April 2009

I'm absolutely buzzing. Sitting here in the press room in Bahrain after the race, tapping out my stories, I get a text from my friend Dave Klafkowski sitting in the Palladium in London to tell me that the ITV F1 coverage of the Brazilian Grand Prix in 2008 has won the BAFTA for best sports programme! It is the third year in a row that the team (of which I was part) has won this most prestigious award.

We had won previously for the coverage of Jenson Button's 2006 Hungarian GP win, for the 2007 Canadian GP show when Lewis

BAHRAIN GRAND PRIX
Bahrain, 57 laps

1. Button	Brawn GP-Mercedes	1h31:48.182
2. Vettel	Red Bull-Renault	+ 7.187
3. Trulli	Toyota	+ 9.170
4. Hamilton	McLaren-Mercedes	+ 22.096
5. Barrichello	Brawn GP-Mercedes	+ 37.779
6. Raikkonen	Ferrari	+ 42.057
7. Glock	Toyota	+ 42.880
8. Alonso	Renault	+ 52.775

DRIVERS' STANDINGS
1. Button   31
2. Barrichello 19
3. Vettel   18
4. Trulli   14.5
5. Glock   12
6. Webber   9.5

CONSTRUCTORS' STANDINGS
1. Brawn GP-Mercedes   50
2. Red Bull-Renault   27.5
3. Toyota   26.5
4. McLaren-Mercedes   13
5. Renault   5
6. Toro Rosso-Ferrari 4

Hamilton won his first race and now the ultimate TV moment in my career has been rewarded with a third straight BAFTA. This is really special because we were up against the BBC's outstanding Olympic coverage and frankly we didn't expect to win. But the BAFTA judges took the view that what happened in that final lap was so extraordinary and the commentary was so spot on, that we deserved the award; we had given the event just the right coverage and soundtrack.

I'm really proud of the work of the entire ITV crew, the production staff from North One TV and the presenters over the 12 years. But I'm especially proud of those last few minutes of programming, which showcased F1 at its absolute finest.

How Ross Brawn has changed Jenson Button
28 April 2009

Jenson Button took his third win of the season on Sunday in fine style. This was a victory which demanded a great deal of care, because he didn't have the fastest car out there on the day, not even on the qualifying day, even though the Brawn had appeared to have the legs of the others in Friday practice.

He also had to be aggressive on the opening lap, to regain the place lost to Lewis Hamilton at the start. F1 fans around the world are now debating whether Button can capitalise on the superb start he has made to the first part of the season and win the world title. He will face a growing challenge from teams like McLaren, Renault and Ferrari, while Toyota and Red Bull are already on his pace.

But I sense a real difference about Jenson this year. I think that Ross Brawn has given him a greater sense of discipline, not just in his driving but in his life as a whole. And in that pass on Hamilton, he showed the importance of giving nothing away, something which characterised Michael Schumacher's driving and Ross Brawn's whole approach to racing.

Button has always had a great talent and a uniquely smooth style. And when he started, he learned the F1 ropes pretty quickly. Let's not forget that this is the man who at the age of 20, on his first visit to Spa, pointed out to the FIA's Charlie Whiting that the 100 metre braking board was in the wrong place on the approach to La Source hairpin. They measured it and found he was correct.

So, behind this rather laid-back facade, a sympathy for precision and discipline has always been there, but many years in bad cars had rather blunted the edge. Also the same lack of discipline and leadership in the technical department at Honda, which caused them to misfire, has been transformed under Brawn's leadership.

I'll give you a small example. Every time Button enters the pits during practice he drives into his pit box with the mechanics in the positions they would be in for a pit stop. He comes in and stops in position. But that is not where it ends. There is a brief pause on the radio and then Andrew Shovlin, Button's race engineer, will say, "ten centimetres out". There is no further comment, no response from Jenson. Sometimes he comes in and you will hear Brawn himself say, "perfect position Jenson".

This precision matters because it means that when Button stops for real in the race, the refuellers will be able to do their job more easily and the stop will be faster. Such attention to detail is the hallmark of Ross Brawn, honed over many years with Michael Schumacher at Ferrari. The ethos at Ferrari was that everyone had to give 100% all the time and if each person could count on the others to do that, they would be successful. It has undoubtedly sharpened up Button's racecraft. He seems very on top of every aspect of the game at the moment.

"I've got no doubts about Jenson's ability to win, " Ross said on Saturday. "The way he is driving, that part is taken care of. It's up to us to produce the performance in the car, do the pit stops, the strategies, and make sure the car is reliable."

Button's driving life has been rather chaotic for much of his F1 career. You may recall the dithering over a possible move back to Williams and the odd situation where he had to buy himself out of his contract. Now after a few years under Richard Goddard's management that side of his life seems to have settled down and become more under control. There is a unity of purpose about every aspect of his life. I've seen it before in racing drivers, when they get into a position to win races they get into the "zone". Button is in the zone right now.

Will Branson put serious money into Brawn?
29 April 2009

There seems to be a division of opinion about what is going on between Brawn GP and Sir Richard Branson's Virgin Group. There are rumours that a deal has been done for this year and next, but there are also strong suggestions coming out of the team that other parties are interested and that Branson should pony up some more serious money if he wishes to go forward.

Branson was in the Bahrain paddock at the weekend, holding a press conference to announce that Rubens Barrichello and Niki Lauda had both paid €200,000 to fly into space on the Virgin Galactic spaceship. Lauda, who is on crutches after a hip replacement, is due to take a turn at flying the craft.

In *The Times* today, Brawn CEO Nick Fry gives a very interesting quote:

"Richard has made an offer. The issue for us is whether or not it is the best offer we can get. We've got between 20 and 25 companies talking to us either about sponsorship or some wanting to buy into the team. Ross and I need to come to the correct decision, not the quick decision."

Branson has a reputation for getting the maximum exposure for the minimum spend. Already the media value to his brand of the exposure from the first four races plus his appearances in Australia and Bahrain is estimated at £10 million, which is likely to be at least ten times what he has invested. That proves to him on the one hand that F1 in general (and Brawn in particular) is a great way to get exposure, but it also shows him that he can achieve it very cheaply. But this is not going down very well with the powers that be in F1, and the Brawn team is now coming to the point where they are asking him to invest serious money for the long term.

The team has a "budget to impress" in Ross Brawn's words, from Honda to get them through the 2009 season, but they need more money to develop the car to stay ahead of the rest and win the world title. They also need money to get started on next year's car.

The word I heard in Bahrain is that Brawn are looking for a three year commitment from any prospective partner. The discussions with Virgin have revolved around the rest of this year and a commitment to fund the development of the 2010 car.

Discussions will of course have been hanging in recent weeks, waiting for the FIA to set the level of the budget cap. Many teams are nervous about sponsors' reactions if the budget is set at £30-50 million, as they fear the sponsors will be asking for the price to come down proportionately.

However the price they pay is not related to the team's needs, it is related to the media value of the exposure they get, based on camera time, press cuttings and so on, something Branson and his team will be all too aware of given their success in that area in the last month.

The budget cap, if it happens, will redefine the business model of F1 and if the price is low enough it may make it attractive for Virgin to consider more than a sponsorship, perhaps to buy an equity stake in the team. F1 teams are set to become profitable under a budget cap, so as an owner/partner you still get your exposure and you make money too. Time will tell.

As Honda, the team was very close to a deal with Emirates Airlines, a deal which was linked to the Earthdreams concept, but it never happened. The team has not been the market leader in attracting sponsors at any time in its history. As BAR they didn't really need sponsors as the whole operation was bankrolled by a tobacco company. When the team became Honda and BAT pulled out, the same attitude prevailed.

Fry and his new commercial team are under pressure to deliver a full roster of sponsors to take the Brawn team forward and make sure that this year's championship-leading performance is not a flash in the pan.

An announcement about Virgin's future involvement is expected at the Spanish Grand Prix in a few weeks' time.

FIA reveals details of budget cap for F1
30 April 2009

The details of the budget cap have been released by the FIA.

The scheme will operate from next season. The level has been set at £40 million with no "glide path" down from a higher figure to a lower one.

It will present teams with an obligation to lay off a significant number of people quickly, which in itself is an expensive exercise.

The FIA has maintained the idea of a two-tier championship, with teams able to spend more if they wish to, but the cost-controlled teams will enjoy greater technical freedom. This will greatly annoy Ferrari and BMW.

The FIA statement reads as follows:

> "From 2010, all teams will have the option to compete with cars built and operated within a stringent cost cap.
>
> The cost cap for 2010 will be £40m per annum. This figure will cover all team expenditure except:
> - Marketing and hospitality;
> - Remuneration for test or race drivers, including any young driver programmes;
> - Fines or penalties imposed by the FIA;
> - Engine costs (for 2010 only);
> - Any expenditure which the team can demonstrate has no influence on its performance in the Championship;
> - Dividends (including any tax thereon) paid from profits relating to participation in the Championship."

Drivers being excluded will drive up their wages. But these may fall under the budget cap in future years. Engines being excluded means an additional £5 million for customer teams and allows the manufacturers some latitude in reshaping their engine departments. Many will be providing customer engines to teams.

The whole plan is aimed at attracting new teams to the series and the field has been increased to 26 cars, so 13 teams can get an entry. Bernie Ecclestone has agreed to give the new teams a share of the prize money (normally they would have to serve a couple of years before getting anything).

> "In addition to the payments which it already makes to the top ten teams in the Championship, Formula One Management,

the commercial rights holder, has agreed to offer participation fees and expenses to the new teams. This includes an annual payment of US$10 million to each team plus free transportation of two chassis and freight up to 10,000kg in weight (not including the two chassis) as well as 20 air tickets (economy class) for each round trip for events held outside Europe.

"To be eligible for this, each new team must qualify as a 'Constructor' and demonstrate that it has the necessary facilities, financial resources and technical competence to compete effectively in Formula One. "

The technical freedoms the capped teams may enjoy are as follows:

> 1. Movable wings, front and rear.

> 2. An engine which is not subject to a rev limit.

The teams will also be allowed unlimited out-of-season track testing with no restrictions on the scale and speed of wind tunnel testing."

To put pressure on the existing teams to comply, the FIA has said that entries must be in soon. Entries are to be submitted during the period 22-29 May 2009. Teams must state in their application whether they wish to compete under cost-cap regulations.

The teams' association, FOTA, is meeting in London on 6 May. Their response will be very interesting, with Ferrari likely to be particularly furious.

Chapter Five
May 2009

Mosley and Montezemolo exchange letters
1 May 2009

The two main protagonists in the war between the FIA and FOTA – and arguably the two largest egos in the piece – are now getting stuck into each other.

In response to the letter Ferrari president Luca di Montezemolo wrote on 28 April to the FIA president expressing concern about having two classes of F1 car and about a possible legal challenge to the budget cap, Max Mosley wrote back the following day, quoting Fiat boss Sergio Marchionne (with whom Montezemolo works closely) and the Italian's belief that in an economic crisis such as our current one only an extreme response will do.

"We are just going to slam the brakes on, cut everything back to essentials. It may be painful, it may be ugly. But if we want to do the right thing for this industry let's do it now. Today my gut instinct is to be truly Draconian." These are Marchionne's words.

Mosley points out that the car industry is in serious difficulty and that F1, as an extension of it, is extremely vulnerable. Honda's departure was a wake-up call and another manufacturer could leave at any moment. "If we are to reduce the risk of the Formula 1 world championship collapsing, we have to allow new teams in. We also have to reduce costs drastically. The matter is therefore extremely urgent."

Responding to Montezemolo's legal threat over rights that have not been respected Mosley writes:

"The only radical elements are those needed to close the gap that would otherwise exist between a low-budget team and other competitors. Thus if Ferrari chooses to continue with an unrestricted budget, the new regulations will not deprive Ferrari of any rights... I do not accept that these proposed regulations compromise any commitment that has been given to Ferrari in the past, unless Ferrari would somehow argue that it is entitled to prevent new competitors from emerging at a time when the sport itself is in danger."

He ends with a flourish, "We are confident (as are our accountants and lawyers) that a budget cap will be enforceable. The cleverest team will win and we would eliminate the need for depressing restrictions on technology, which the existing teams are discussing with a view to reducing costs. I hope Ferrari will take the lead in agreeing the cost-cap mechanism, thus freeing its engineers to work and preserving its shareholders' money."

Mosley has always wanted three things to change: to see the playing field levelled so small teams can compete with big teams, to have full grids, and finally some control over costs, which he has always felt were out of control, long before the credit crunch hit the global economy.

What he has done here, along with his technical strategy guru Tony Purnell, is to take advantage of the car industry's troubles to create a window for killing those three birds with one stone. The two-class F1 is not ideal for anyone, but Mosley is calculating that no manufacturer will go for the uncapped option because it would be unjustifiable to shareholders.

Meanwhile the five independent teams, Williams, Red Bull, Toro Rosso, Brawn and Force India all welcome the budget cap at the £40 million level because to them this means survival, profit and the chance to compete against the big boys. For them it's Christmas.

The teams formed their own association, FOTA, to represent their rights, but here FOTA is in big trouble because the five independents are on a collision course with the manufacturers, so Max has also achieved a fourth aim, to undermine FOTA.

Many people dislike his methods, but think about it this way: if F1 didn't exist and you were Ferrari or any other manufacturer and someone came to you and said, "I've got a great idea for a racing series; we'll have 17 races in key markets around the world, with great TV packages giving your brand a media value in the hundreds of millions per year, but it will only cost £40 million and it is capped. You can innovate within that figure and beat the others."

I'm sure if you started with a clean sheet of paper, in other words, you might well go for the deal on that basis. But it's hard to accept the Mosley/Purnell vision for F1 because we come from an era of £200 million budgets. But why does it need to cost £200 million to win?

Shouldn't Ferrari continue to win races? If you have something very good and you distil it to its core strengths, you end up with something sensational. So surely the 350 best people at Ferrari must be the equal of - or better than - the 350 at any of the other teams?

Mind you, this is all happening at a time when races are being won by the two independent teams, Brawn and Red Bull. Most people find this very refreshing and a good thing for F1. However it's really hard to know which way to go on this one, because it represents a huge cultural shift in F1. You can see Ferrari's point in that they believe that they have right, the law and history on their side.

Whatever your opinion, it is likely that there will be a summer of messy legal challenges, which would throw the 2010 season into chaos. Ferrari will not go quietly and have gathered the other manufacturers around them for a council of war. They make the engines, of course, so the independents are dependent on them.

That is why Cosworth is sitting on the sidelines, waiting.

F1 can survive without Ferrari, says Mosley
2 May 2009

Yesterday I met with Max Mosley for a long interview which is published in today's *Financial Times*. He was in London briefly following this week's World Motorsport Council meeting when the £40 million budget cap for 2010 was voted through. I asked Mosley whether F1 could survive without Ferrari.

"It could," he said. "It would be very sad to lose them. They've been in the sport since the start, but if it's a choice between that and a situation doomed to failure and which would collapse F1... We are not going to bend over backwards to keep them."

Mosley described the budget cap move as "by far the biggest development in my time in the sport". He was confident though that this is a time for action, not for wait and see, as the economy struggles to recover from global recession and car companies collectively are losing £1 billion a month. But he accepts that it might go wrong and that this summer could see a damaging stand-off between some teams and the FIA.

"If you are trying to make big changes things can go wrong," said Mosley. "We may have a very damaging conflict, it's possible, but we are prepared for that. We'd tough it out. We've got very little room to negotiate, but the message I'm getting from the boards of two or three of the manufacturers is that if you can keep us in F1 so that the cheque we write is not more than €25 million, you can consider this a pretty permanent arrangement."

In recent years the manufacturer-backed teams, like Honda, BMW, Toyota, Mercedes and Renault have fuelled an arms-race of costs, but the boards of those car companies take a different view, according to Mosley, especially now that the economic picture has deteriorated.

"We have contacts with the boards other than through the teams. The teams spin to the boards. The CEO hasn't got the time, knowledge or expertise to question it. But now because they are all [short of money] to throw away tens of millions on F1 is not acceptable. I hope and think that when a team goes to its board and says, 'I want to go to war with the FIA, because I want to be able to spend £100 million more than the FIA want me to spend, then the board will say 'Why can't you spend £40 million if the other teams can do it?' "

Mosley believes that Formula 1 has "gone down the wrong track", with the emphasis on endless costly developments, rather than genuine innovation. He believes that the budget cap reverses that trend.

"The cleverest team is going to win, not the richest. It's manifestly fair because it literally is the one who makes the best invention who will succeed. Invention is cheap, it's refinement that is expensive and F1 is now refinement-orientated. It's probably our fault for allowing rules to develop in such a way that refinement is the means of progress rather than invention."

Raikkonen in London ahead of big weekend for Ferrari
6 May 2009

Kimi Raikkonen will be in Regent's Street, London, this morning, opening the new Ferrari store. It's a big site, I went past it yesterday and it's full of Ferrari branded goodies.

It's amazing to think that it's a year since Raikkonen last won a Grand Prix. He dominated the Spanish GP last season from pole, but since then he's failed to make the top step. He would probably have won in Canada if he had not been hit in the pit lane by Lewis Hamilton and he was on target in France until his exhaust started burning a hole in the bodywork of his car.

"It was one of my best weekends with Ferrari," he says on the Ferrari website. "Pole, win and fastest lap. A driver never loses his taste for victory and I want to try it again as soon as possible."

Raikkonen did a great job in Bahrain, squeezing the absolute maximum out of the Ferrari there, putting to rest any doubts about whether he still has the motivation. He was unlucky at the end not to nick fifth place off Rubens Barrichello.

There is the spectre of Alonso in the background, with well-informed Italian colleagues assuring me that an agreement is in place with the Spaniard, just as it was with Kimi for almost a year before it became public in late 2006. The deal is for 2011, but may be brought forward to 2010 if Kimi underperforms or wants out early.

The president of Santander was very high profile in Bahrain, spending a lot of time around the Ferrari area. The Spanish bank is due to come on stream as a sponsor of Ferrari next year. Santander accompanied Alonso to McLaren in 2007 for his ill-fated season there.

F1 teams in race against time
7 May 2009

The FOTA teams met yesterday in London to discuss developments in the 2010 rules and to co-ordinate a response to the FIA's introduction of the £40 million budget cap for next season.

The statement, as usual, was fairly bland and uninformative, but did hint at the seriousness of the situation, as FOTA sees it:

"FOTA held a positive and constructive meeting and agreed to continue working together in a methodical manner for the definition of further cost-reduction in 2010 and 2011, progressing along the path begun in 2008. FOTA has concerns with the decisions taken at the last WMSC meeting regarding the 2010 regulations and therefore asks to begin urgent consultations with the FIA."

The statement was issued yesterday evening and made no reference to the death of FIA president Max Mosley's 39-year-old son Alexander, from a suspected drug overdose, announced earlier in the day. Mosley has cancelled a planned visit to Spain this weekend for the Grand Prix, where he was due to hold a press conference. His son's death is bound to dominate his thoughts and his agenda for a period of time.

The teams have been given a one-week window later this month in which they have to enter the 2010 championship. So it is a matter of urgency for them to decide on a co-ordinated negotiating position and to see if they can get the FIA around the table to smooth out the plans for 2010 to make them work for more of the teams.

Basically the teams are all agreed that you cannot have two-tier F1, with some cars running budget capped and others running outside it with fewer technical freedoms. But beyond that there is a split, with half the teams, the independents, in favour of a budget cap at around £40 million and the other half with a range of objections.

The rules for 2010 also include the winner-takes-all points system, which had been voted through for this season, but the teams had objected that their unanimous vote was needed to bring it through at such short notice and the FIA backed down, declaring that it would be deferred to 2010. It is now enshrined in the rules as follows:

"The Formula One World Championship Drivers' Title will be awarded to the driver who has been classified first in the greatest number of races, all official results from the Championship season being taken into account.

"Points will be awarded to all drivers in accordance with Article 6.4 below and, in the event that two or more drivers win an equal number of races, the driver with the greatest number of points will be awarded the Drivers' Title."

* * *

In fact it turned out that the points statement was a typing error, a cut and paste mistake which left the winner-takes-all system in the rules, despite the fact that the FIA had agreed to take it out. The standard points system remains in place to this day and will be in place for 2010, as things stand.

* * *

Piquet looks for the arm around the shoulder
8 May 2009

I went along to Nelson Piquet's press briefing yesterday afternoon here in Barcelona. The poor lad is under some pressure at the moment, with speculation that he has just this race and Monaco to save his seat. So far this season he has not impressed, struggling particularly in qualifying. Twice 15th on the grid, twice 17th, he admitted that lack of testing had caused his problems.

"Not getting pre-season (testing), not running low fuel, and then suddenly, when you put everything together, you can't get the maximum out of it. Or you push too much and you end up overdriving the car. I think I need to get qualifying sorted. My strong point always in my career was qualifying. Of course it doesn't mean much in lower categories, but I have been the driver with the most pole positions all the years. This year I'm struggling a little bit more. Last year it was okay because it was my first year. But this year I should have been much better in qualifying."

Piquet is one of those drivers who needs miles under his belt in order to perform. He has to play himself in, can't just turn it on straight away. It is no surprise that they have kept him in the car for this race and Monaco because both are difficult tracks for a new guy to come in and master on a race weekend. Piquet also knows this place really well, so if he's going to do it anywhere it will be here. What is happening to him is an illustration of the fact that in F1 nowadays you have to be adaptable and nail it first time, as drivers like Sebastian Vettel do. With no testing during the season, drivers like the young Brazilian will become less attractive to teams.

In an amusing exchange, when he was asked whether he just needed an arm around the shoulder, a bit of a cuddle, he said "I think that's also a part of it. There are a lot of people in the team who don't like being cuddling *(sic)*. But the important people that we work with day to day, the engineers, they are trying their best. I'm very happy to have them because they are trying everything possible to get me back into qualifying rhythm. I think I need to get my rhythm in qualifying back and once that's sorted in the races I'm more than capable of doing it."

Piquet has been given a lot of help and support. Now the pressure is really on, he has to deliver on Saturday in qualifying.

Button wins in Spain, Barrichello and Vettel lose
10 May 2009

This is starting to remind me of 1992 when Nigel Mansell took a very good car and dominated the championship with it, after years of it seeming that the world title might elude him. The difference is that then the Williams Renault was massively superior to the rest and Mansell was far faster than team-mate Patrese.

This situation may look the same, but it's not. The Brawn is not a huge step ahead of the rest, in fact the Red Bull is every bit as fast and has now squandered two good chances to win, in Bahrain and Barcelona. As for the team-mate rivalry, Button did the business over Barrichello in qualifying, but the race was Rubens's to lose after the first stint. The team switched the strategies and the race went Jenson's way.

After the race Rubens came out with an extraordinary statement, saying in a live interview on US Speed TV channel, "If I get a whiff that Ross favoured Jenson today I will hang up my helmet immediately. But I don't think he would do that."

A lot of people here suspect that Barrichello might have been on the wrong end of things today. The original plan was for both drivers to do three pit stops, because the computer said it was faster. But as a tactic it is fraught with the problem of traffic.

Button pitted first, having lost the lead at the start to Barrichello and being switched to a two-stop plan, with a long middle stint. The reason for this was that he was going to emerge behind Rosberg anyway in a very heavy Williams and this would have wrecked his strategy if he had stayed on three stops.

Barrichello pitted a lap later but was kept on a three-stop. He rejoined behind Massa and Vettel, but both of them pitted the next lap so he was back in the lead two laps after his stop, able to motor in clear air. Then his second set of tyres worked well but the third set not so well and he lost the vital ground he needed. He saw what should have been a certain win slip away from him.

Sebastian Vettel also lost the race today. The Red Bull driver once again spent almost the entire race stuck behind another car, in this case Felipe Massa's. Massa got him off the start line and that was it. Only in the final laps when Massa was running out of fuel and had to slow down did Vettel get past him.

Red Bull has had a marginally faster car than the Brawn in the last two races and yet Vettel has ended up doing the races at someone else's pace because he's been behind a slower car. Here I believe he would have won the race, especially as his car was the only one which could get the hard tyres working properly in the final stint. "I was on the wrong strategy," said a disconsolate Vettel afterwards.

But the mistake was made on Saturday. What Red Bull have not done is fuel him a little lighter to get pole and then be sure of getting a clear run at the front. The Red Bull is a faster qualifying car than the Brawn, so why not use it and get to the front of the grid, from where he could control things? The way they have done it, he's twice now been vulnerable to KERS cars, Hamilton in Bahrain and Massa here, and both times they have wrecked his race.

An interesting cameo in the Red Bull area after the race: someone close to Mark Webber, who drove brilliantly to leapfrog both Massa and Vettel and grab a podium, said, "I'm glad someone here is happy", implying that the place was like a morgue because the chosen one had not got the anticipated result...

SPANISH GRAND PRIX
Barcelona 66 laps

1. Button	Brawn GP-Mercedes	1h37:19.202
2. Barrichello	Brawn GP-Mercedes	+ 13.056
3. Webber	Red Bull-Renault	+ 13.924
4. Vettel	Red Bull-Renault	+ 18.941
5. Alonso	Renault	+ 43.166
6. Massa	Ferrari	+ 50.827
7. Heidfeld	BMW Sauber	+ 52.312
8. Rosberg	Williams-Toyota	+ 1:05.211

DRIVERS' STANDINGS
1. Button   41
2. Barrichello   27
3. Vettel   23
4. Webber   15.5
5. Trulli   14.5
6. Glock   12

CONSTRUCTORS' STANDINGS
1. Brawn GP-Mercedes   68
2. Red Bull-Renault   38.5
3. Toyota   26.5
4. McLaren-Mercedes   13
5. Renault   9
6. BMW Sauber   6

In the Easyjet set with Ross Brawn and Co
11 May 2009

Vijay Mallya is bobbing in the harbour on his motor yacht, Flavio Briatore will have zoomed off in his private jet, like most of the drivers, but the winning team boss of today's Grand Prix was on the Easyjet flight to Luton with his team, plus Red Bull, Force India, me and a load of sunburned, happy fans.

Most of them couldn't believe their eyes that Ross Brawn was checking in for the same Easyjet flight as them and he had to pose for photos with many of them. His only token bit of elitism - he paid €12 for Speedy Boarding!

Ross has always been a team player when it comes to travel. A number of times in the past when my family has been on holiday in Italy in the summer I've cadged a lift on the Ferrari charter and Ross and Jean Todt always used to travel with the engineers and mechanics on the same plane. It's part of the team-building ethic, which also includes sending different members of the team up on to the podium, to allow them to feel that special buzz and to motivate them to work hard to achieve it again.

Anyway, on the way out on Thursday morning the Easyjet plane was half-full of hungover Barcelona fans on their way home after beating Chelsea in the Champions League football match. Ross was sitting next to a guy who must have weighed a good 20 stone and who had clearly been in a bar all night.

Tonight Brawn was on good form, relieved to have won another race and to have negotiated all the potential little problems, surprised that Red Bull hadn't done more with pit strategy to try to get Vettel away from Massa. The atmosphere on the plane was good. The captain in his welcome speech congratulated the team on its success and wished them many more. The Red Bull guys rolled their eyes.

Brawn has now won 11 trophies in the five races so far and Jenson Button has dropped only four points from a possible 45. They are making it look Easy.

Williams question "inconsistent" Rosberg
11 May 2009

I'm intrigued by the comments coming out of the Williams camp over the last 24 hours, regarding Nico Rosberg.

First, at the top of yesterday's press release after the race they said, "Inconsistency compromised a strong strategy and left Nico in P8 and with one point at race end."

Then lower down, Patrick Head says, "Nico's pace in the first stint was initially good, but we then struggled to maintain consistency, so we will have to investigate that."

Today comes a debrief document from the team, in which technical director Sam Michael says:

"Nico's lap times were somewhat inconsistent, yes, and we are now looking carefully through all of the data and bodywork parts to determine what caused that."

Williams's frustration is evident; they lie 8th in the constructors' championship with a scant 4.5 points, despite being one of the teams who started the season with the advantage of a double diffuser.

Sam Michael goes on to say, "Even if we think we have a faster car than how we currently stand in the table, the constructors' order is what the overall performance of our team is measured by."

This is all finessed with layers of PR gloss, but reading between the lines I think Williams are a bit fed up with Rosberg's performance this year. In his defence, as far as the inconsistency is concerned, I heard last night before I left the track that Rosberg had suffered some problem with the floor of the car, which may have affected him in certain corners around the Barcelona track and resulted in him struggling to turn in consistent times. I look forward to the findings of their current investigations into the car.

The simple fact is that Rosberg hasn't really been pulling up trees this year. I've heard it suggested that if someone like Fernando Alonso were in that car he would have scored podiums with it, but who's to know?

Let's take a look at Nico's race and see what the team is referring to. He starts the race on Sunday from 9th on the grid, but took advantage of the chaos at the first corner to move up to 7th. His lap times do not come down like the other front-running drivers, a lap of 1m 24.2 is followed by a 1m 25.0. A few laps later a 1m 24.1 is followed by a 1m 25.9. No traffic is involved. He pits on lap 25 and the second stint is more consistent, working his way down through the 1m 24s to the 1m 23s. There is often three or four tenths of disparity between laps, however. He has lost time and later in the race Nick Heidfeld in the BMW gets in front of him, at the second pit stops.

The BMW is at least two tenths slower than the Williams, so this is an irritant. In Bahrain it will have exasperated the team that Rosberg, with a significant package of upgrades, was only two tenths faster than Nakajima in qualifying. The impression is of a driver who is struggling to make things happen in his fourth season in F1.

I remember a few years ago, when one of the drivers wasn't pulling his weight to the extent Patrick expected, he said, "We are deep in Boutsen territory", referring to Thierry Boutsen, who had plenty of days when he wasn't able to perform. I'm not saying for a second that they are in 'Boutsen territory" now, but Rosberg is certainly under scrutiny. That message is coming through loud and clear.

* * *

Rosberg got the message and went on a long run of consistent points finishes, scoring 25 points in the next six races, which completely turned around the perception of him, even making him a hot property on the driver market.

* * *

Ferrari threatens to quit F1
12 May 2009

Ferrari today decided to test Max Mosley's assertion that "Formula 1 can survive without Ferrari".

It issued a strongly worded statement following a meeting of the board of directors, which said that it would not enter the 2010 F1 world championship if the rules voted through by the FIA World Council on 29 April are not changed It noted that the April meeting had been convened to hear a disciplinary matter (the McLaren liar-gate scandal) and that the decisions taken there brought into being a two-tier system of rules "based on arbitrary technical rules and parameters".

The statement goes on to say that "if this is [to be the] regulatory framework for Formula 1 in the future, then the reasons underlying Ferrari's uninterrupted participation in the world championship over the last 60 years... would come to a close.

"The board also went on to express its disappointment about the methods adopted by the FIA in taking decisions of such a serious nature and its refusal to effectively reach an understanding with constructors and teams."

Ferrari argues that the rules of governance that have contributed to the development of F1 over the last 25 years have been disregarded, as have the binding contractual obligations between Ferrari and the FIA itself regarding the stability of the regulations. But Ferrari's beef goes beyond just saying that they want the rules on budget caps to be dropped. They want to use this episode to force a review of the way the sport is governed by the FIA.

Bernie Ecclestone worked hard over the weekend in Barcelona to get the teams to think about a way forward on this. Basically the manufacturers are all lined up behind Ferrari. Toyota's John Howett paved the way for today's announcement by saying effectively the same thing and now we will see if BMW, Mercedes and Renault follow Ferrari out of the trenches and declare that they too will quit F1 if the conditions don't change.

Ferrari saying that they will quit F1 is a massive statement, the consequences of which will resonate all over the world and seriously undermine the commercial stability of the sport. It is a real shame for all parties that it has come to this. As they say, their participation in F1 has lasted an unbroken 60 years and although they have threatened to withdraw in the past behind closed doors, to come out with such a strong public statement is in itself damaging for the credibility of the sport, even if the threat is not ultimately carried through.

Ferrari president Luca di Montezemolo was due to meet Max Mosley anyway later this week in London, but he has decided to massively up the ante ahead of that meeting.

In the interests of Ferrari and the sport, both men will have to climb down from their current positions. But there is more to this than merely hammering out a deal on budget cuts. Ferrari has gone further and questioned the governance of the sport and the last two lines of the statement are heavily loaded:

"The chairman of the board of directors [Montezemolo] was mandated to evaluate the most suitable ways and methods to protect the company's interests."

This has several meanings in one. It means that they are looking into a legal challenge because they believe that "binding contractual obligations" have been breached. These refer to a veto right which Ferrari negotiated into its deal when it broke ranks with the other manufacturers in early 2005 and signed up to stay in F1 until 2012. Also it means that they are evaluating other sporting series, whether joining an existing one, like Le Mans, or starting a new one with the other manufacturers. This then is a test of which is the stronger brand. Is it Ferrari or is it Formula 1?

As an aside, it would be very interesting to know whether some broadcasters and promoters have a condition in their contracts with Bernie Ecclestone's FOM that certain specific teams have to be in the field, one of which would surely be Ferrari.

When the manufacturers were thinking about that breakaway series in 2004-05, I know that this was discussed as a way of TV companies being sure that they were going to be showing the right series.

Ferrari: "We made F1 great"
14 May 2009

As the pressure builds in the powerplay between the FIA and the manufacturers, led by Ferrari, the Scuderia continue to push the idea that F1 is what it is today because of their unbroken participation over 60 years. On the official Ferrari website they have posted a piece called, "The pride of making F1 great" and they go on to list all the great moments which make up the sport's history in which Ferrari was the central protagonist.

The intro to the piece reads:

"Since the year 1950, when the modern Formula 1 world championship was held for the first time, Ferrari has been part of it as a player, approaching opportunities and difficulties with sporting spirit. The Scuderia Ferrari is the only team that participated in every championship. It is the only team that conquered 16 constructors' world titles, 15 drivers' titles and 206 victories.

"That is why the Scuderia is loved and respected all over the world. Loved by many of its friends and fans, respected by its competitors."

The threat to race somewhere else is central here, as is the "DNA question" - to what extent can you differentiate the DNA of Ferrari from the DNA of F1?

Whatever the outcome of this - and I am virtually certain a deal will be done for them to stay in F1 - it has been a useful exercise in reminding everyone of Ferrari's importance and its brand values.

I was in the Ferrari store yesterday in Regent's Street, shooting a report for Italian RAI TV on this story. It sits on that street alongside Jaeger, Hamley's, Hugo Boss and Apple. Ferrari has decided to really leverage its brand and make some money out of what is one of the world's most famous and distinctive names. When you look at how the team has pushed the button on licensing, marketing and merchandising in recent years, led by head of brand Danny Behar, who did a similar job for Red Bull for many years, you see that this current exercise in challenging the FIA could also be regarded as an exercise in reinforcing the Ferrari brand. We have all been forced to reflect in recent days on what Ferrari means to us. People might be more inclined, as a result of that reflection, to buy a pair of Ferrari-branded Puma trainers than they were last week.

Did Ferrari make F1 great? Or is it the other way around? Or could both statements be true, proving the veracity of Bernie Ecclestone's view that Ferrari and F1 is the perfect marriage?

Next week this debate – or should that be debacle - will move on to another brand F1 cannot do without: Monaco. It's the only track which does more for F1 than F1 does for it.

Why Lewis Hamilton has fallen out of love with F1
16 May 2009

You will have seen some of the interviews Lewis Hamilton did this week, on Reuters, in *The Times* and on the BBC.

The Times one caught my eye because it was an open expression of regret that Formula 1 has become a job and that he does not enjoy the political environment around him.

Hamilton has slotted into the space left vacant by Michael Schumacher in Formula 1 - clearly he is massively talented, but seemingly unloved by his fellow drivers and always finding himself tangled up in controversies. Senna occupied that space before Schumacher.

The Times interview reveals the state of mind of the driver in the third season of his F1 career. He is weary of the politics, no longer enjoys the banter with the media, he is on his guard, feeling caged and also unfulfilled because his car isn't fast enough to get him into the game.

"It doesn't feel so good," he said, "getting up in the morning and knowing you can't win that weekend no matter how hard you drive or how good a job you or the team does.

"It's hard to take but it's a fact and you have to deal with it. You just have to adjust your expectations and find new goals."

In other words Hamilton now finds himself in the same position as most drivers in F1, who have no chance of winning a race, even though their career up to that level was probably gilded with victories and championships. Hamilton tactlessly described some of these drivers as "the monkeys at the back" last season and it is unsurprising if few have any sympathy for him now.

In Spain last weekend he found out just how it felt to be at the back, lapped by Jenson Button in the closing stages of the race.

"I have known Jenson since I was ten years old," continues Hamilton. "He has had some tough, tough years and I think I can appreciate even more after this year exactly how he felt. I have a huge amount of respect for how he dealt with it all."

What is happening at the moment with Hamilton is that he is having to rebuild all his relationships. Imagine a telephone switchboard, with loads of leads plugged in all over the place. Well, Hamilton has unplugged all those leads and is now taking great care over how he plugs each one back in again. It is a root and branch reconstruction of some of the key relationships which make up the ebb and flow of his F1 life: his relationship with his team after the lying episode in Melbourne and the human damage which ensued, his relationship with the media, his relationship with his fellow drivers.

The media one is a perpetual battle. Hamilton will have hated being made to go in front of the press in Malaysia to apologise for lying but it worked well and most of the media respected him for it. But the trouble is now that whenever he finds himself in the middle of another controversy, there will be the inevitable enquiry, "Are you going to apologise, Lewis?"

Exactly the same thing happened with Schumacher. He tired of dealing with the media and always refused to give them what they wanted when they made demands on him. He was stubborn like that and I bet Lewis will be the same.

Despite in later years growing to hate his dealings with the media, Schumacher was always very professional and did what he had to do, always gave an answer. He found a coping mode, which got him through to the end of his career. He was extremely well advised by Sabine Kehm, a former F1 editor on *Die Welt*, the German equivalent of *The Times*. Lewis has his Dad and the McLaren media department to help him, but no one who's done the Fleet Street nasty stuff and who is there to look after his interests alone. He's lost out because of that, no question.

Lately he's been trying the disrespectful grunt or monosyllabic answer, particularly to the Fleet Street tabloid contingent, and it has got him nowhere. They are a thick-skinned lot, however, and he will be a big story as long as he stays in F1. I am sure Lewis will slot into "Schumacher media mode" too, once he's worked out how to plug all those leads back in again, deciding who are the good guys and who are the bad.

To be reworking relationships across so many sectors at once does seem to be taking a lot on. At least he has the mental space and time for it this year. He's not under pressure for the title race. The car isn't going to give him much this season; it will improve, but it's one of those McLarens that doesn't really work, so he'll be "polishing a turd" as racing folk have it, for the rest of the season. Let's hope the same cannot be said for his relationship rebuilding exercise.

Mosley expects half the field not to enter 2010 championship
18 May 2009

FIA president Max Mosley has said that he expects perhaps half the current F1 field not to lodge an entry by the deadline of 29 May.

Tomorrow the Ferrari injunction against the FIA over the process by which it drew up the 2010 rules package will be heard at the High Court in Paris. Ferrari believes that the FIA has not respected a right of veto on F1 rule changes, which it negotiated back in 2005. If the injunction succeeds it opens the way to a full legal challenge of the way the rules for next season were drawn up.

"I think that we will probably get anywhere between three and six teams by the deadline, depending," Mosley told *Autosport*. "After that they become a late entry and if there is a space they can take it, and if there isn't space they cannot.

"They have to make up their minds what they want to do. If they want to continue racing in F1, then they can come and talk. And if they want to go and do something else, then they have got to start making a car."

Several teams are believed to be thinking seriously about entering a team in the 2010 world championships, including Lola, Prodrive, USGPE and GP2 Team I Sport.

One of the options for the manufacturers is to start their own series and, as it happens, they commissioned a detailed study into the feasibility of this when they were formed into the Grand Prix Manufacturers Association a few years ago. But that was at the height of the economic cycle, when car sales and media rights were at a peak.

Now the landscape is very different. It is a huge undertaking to start a new series and there couldn't be a worse time to do it. The manufacturers involved in F1 all have far bigger problems to deal with than investing heavily to start their own series. This is the calculation Mosley and Bernie Ecclestone are making.

They could join forces with an existing series, but in either case one of the hardest parts would be getting a really good television package together, because without that there would be no sponsors and no wider media interest. The deals for F1 are signed up well in advance and with many of the world's leading broadcasters, like the BBC. A split, whereby Ferrari and other manufacturers race in one series and Brawn, Force India, Williams and others are in another would not work for either series. F1 would be a pale shadow of its former self and the new series, despite Ferrari's presence, would be quite a tough sell in the current TV market.

I don't think it will come to this, but there is no doubt that we are passing through a very painful moment for the sport.

* * *

Ferrari lost the court action, on the grounds that it had not taken the opportunity to exercise its veto at the decisive World Council meeting in April.

* * *

Ferrari ridicule new F1 teams
20 May 2009

On the official Ferrari website there is an extraordinary piece, posted today, which has a major dig at the calibre of teams lining up to join Formula 1 next season under the new budget cap rules. The tone is very disparaging. Under the headline "Formula 1 or GP3?" the following piece appeared, quoted verbatim:

> "Maranello, 20 May - They couldn't almost believe their eyes, the men at women (sic) working at Ferrari, when they read the papers this morning and found the names of the teams, declaring that they have the intention to race in Formula 1 in the next year.

> "Looking at the list, which leaked yesterday from Paris, you can't find a very famous name, one of those one has to spend

400 Euros per person for a place on the grandstand at a GP (plus the expenses for the journey and the stay..). Wirth Research, Lola, USF1, Epsilon Euskadi, RML, Formtech, Campos, iSport: these are the names of the teams, which should compete in the two-tier Formula 1 wanted by Mosley. Can a World Championship with teams like them - with due respect - can have the same value as today's Formula 1, where Ferrari, the big car manufacturers and teams, who created the history of this sport, compete? Wouldn't it be more appropriate to call it Formula GP3?"

This was posted before the Paris court rejected Ferrari's application for an injunction against the 2010 rules, but it has certainly upped the ante. Ferrari is deliberately stoking up the controversy - remember on their site last week was a long piece about how "Ferrari made F1 great".

The FIA's statement today is as much a response to this latest posting on the Ferrari site as it is to the verdict of the Paris court:

"No competitor should place their interests above those of the sport in which they compete. The FIA, the teams and our commercial partners will now continue to work to ensure the well-being of Formula One in 2010 and beyond."

Button gets into the champion's mindset
21 May 2009

I wasn't surprised to hear Jenson Button say that racing is dominating his life at the moment.

Button is like many drivers who have found themselves in with a chance of winning the world title. Presented with an unexpected opportunity to fulfil his lifetime's ambition, Button is finding that he can think of little else between races.

"I'm probably a right boring bastard at the moment, I really am," he said.

The Englishman has always had a relaxed air about him and in the years when things were not going so well, he found it easy to switch off between races. But beneath the relaxed facade there is an intensity about him; he was always unsettled by not being competitive. He appears to be wearing his current situation quite easily, but it's clearly taking over his life.

"It's different because things are going well and you want to be thinking about how you can improve. When things aren't going so well, you know you need to improve the car and where you are, but you also need to get away from the racing, to forget about it for a few days. At the moment, that's not possible.

"This season is weird because after the last couple of races I've won, I've obviously enjoyed the weekend, but I wake up on the Monday morning and I'm already thinking about the next race.

"It's quite a strange feeling, very different to the rest of my Formula 1 career, winning four races out of five, but you do get used to it very quickly. I will never forget how difficult it can get, how tough it can get, but when you're winning, finishing second is a disappointment.

"Over the last few weeks, I've been non-stop thinking about the next race, running through it in my mind, getting all the data. It's been quite a stressful few weeks. You wouldn't think so, but in a way it is more stressful."

Michael Schumacher lived in this mental state for the best part of 12 years. It's hard not to become obsessive-compulsive in that position.

Racing is a kind of controlled chaos, because there are so many variables at play, especially at the sharp end of Formula 1. A driver always wants to try to master every aspect, control every situation, to bring it under his control, to dominate. In this Button will have been influenced by the mentality of Ross Brawn, who knows all about maintaining competitiveness and giving nothing away.

The scene in Monaco
22 May 2009

While we wait for F1's *"grandes fromages"* to have their summit meetings and decide what kind of spectacle we are going to see next year and beyond in Formula 1, I thought a brief colour post might be in order.

For the first time in years I'm not staying in Monaco for the race. I'm in Villefranche, which is 20 minutes west by train. They have a fantastic train service here with double-decker trains whizzing you along the coastline. Monaco railway station is a 10-minute walk from the paddock and the media centre.

On my way in I passed a series of posters on the wall which stopped me in my tracks; they are Marlboro adverts. You get so used to not seeing any kind of tobacco advertising any more that to see these bold posters of a tattooed Kimi Raikkonen with his car really grab you. This is Monaco, a law unto itself.

This year's Monaco GP is definitely affected by the credit crunch. Chatting to the locals in the market it seems that everything is 20% down this year; ticket sales, hotel bookings, restaurants etc. There are lots of €300 grandstand seats still available.

The boats in the harbour are credit-crunch specification too. There are some nice ones out there, but not the mega-craft we have seen in recent years. I think part of it is the desire to be seen to be doing the right thing. A lot of sponsors take big boats here normally, but in the current climate they don't want to be seen to be living it up.

Ironically the team bosses do have their boats here, like Flavio Briatore, who's Force Blue is playing host to Bernie Ecclestone and Jean Alesi this weekend. It is available for weekly charter the rest of the year for a fee slightly north of £200,000. This afternoon it is also the venue for the FOTA meeting at 2pm. They will have to cover a lot of ground quickly as they are due at the Royal Automobile Club at 4pm to meet Max Mosley and Bernie Ecclestone. It's a good ten minutes from Flav's boat to the club.

One of my Swiss colleagues has pointed out to me that Ferrari has been in F1 for 60 years, but in that time it has not taken part in every race. Apparently they have missed 27 races mostly due to strikes and indus-trial action in the 1960s. But the funniest bit is that they missed the first ever race, the 1950 British Grand Prix, because they weren't happy with the start money! So in a way nothing has really changed.

Bernie Ecclestone has come out today to say that Ferrari cannot pull out before 2012 because of the binding agreement they signed in 2005, part of which was the celebrated right of veto. The French court agreed with Ferrari that this was still in place and the flip-side of that is that Ferrari is committed to stay for three more seasons.

"We would always respect our contracts," Ecclestone said. "And all the teams that have signed contracts with us would expect us to respect them, and we would expect the same from Ferrari. They are saying they are going to walk, we are saying we hope they respect their contract."

I work now for RAI, the Italian TV station, and I was interested to see that the boss of RAI sport, Massimo de Luca, told *La Gazzetta dello Sport* that if Ferrari wasn't in the game they would want to review their contract with Ecclestone: "If Ferrari leaves F1, along with other major manufacturers, then I can guarantee you that RAI, along with all the main TV companies, would take legal action to review our contract."

Alonso starts talking about Ferrari
23 May 2009

There is a fantastic interview with Fernando Alonso in *La Gazzetta dello Sport* today, in which he gently moves closer to talking about Ferrari and his possible move there. It is another important landmark along the way to this partnership being announced.

According to Pino Allievi, the number one writer on the paper, Alonso has moved to a house on the border between Switzerland and Italy, near Lugano. He spoke about the affection he has for Italy and Italians: "As a Spaniard I feel at ease with Italians," he said. "We have a lot of shared culture and character. We have identical feelings."

As for Ferrari, he started talking about the team and was asked how he imagined life would be as part of it. "It's difficult to imagine from the outside. I can only say that when we race in Bahrain the circuit is full of Ferrari banners. You go to China and it's the same. I see Ferrari as a symbol. At the moment I'm driving for Renault, where we are doing a great job. I only think about winning, the rest we'll have to wait and see."

The word I'm hearing is that these next few races are pretty important for Kimi Raikkonen. Although he has a contract for 2010, the suggestion is that he has certain criteria to meet and that an agreement, which is in place with Alonso for 2011, has a clause which could bring it forward to 2010. The next couple of months will be decisive.

One GP driver I spoke to recently said that in the briefings and at moments when the drivers are all together, Kimi seems not to care any more. It's as if he's just going through the motions. It's a shame if this is true, as Raikkonen is one of the most exciting and most talented drivers in F1. However the Italian media has started treating him with a little less respect, referring to him as "Forrest Gump" earlier this weekend, whilst today's *Gazzetta* piece looks to me like a preparation of the ground for Alonso and the future, in a very Italian sort of way.

Ferrari went for Raikkonen in 2006 rather than Alonso because Jean Todt, the boss at the time, had fallen out with Alonso over a test driving agreement in 2001, which Alonso went back on. Now Todt has gone and the feeling in Ferrari is quite different.

Alonso also shed a little more light on what happened at McLaren. Asked what question he would ask Ron Dennis if he had the chance he said, "I would ask him, 'Why didn't you listen to me?' ".

On relations with Lewis Hamilton he said: "I spoke to him when we were team-mates, in Turkey. I said, 'We are fighting for the world title, one against the other, we both want to win, but we also have to find a way to work together.' It was a frank discussion, very open. In reality, he wasn't the problem. The team was."

Button triumphs in Monaco Grand Prix
24 May 2009

Jenson Button did another first-class job to win the Monaco Grand Prix from pole position today. He was followed home by Rubens Barrichello and Kimi Raikkonen, who gave Ferrari their first podium of the season.

Barrichello got the jump on Raikkonen at the start, which was crucial for the outcome of the race as it kept the Ferraris from challenging at the end of the first stint when their tyres were in better condition than the Brawns.

Both Brawns started on the supersoft tyre, the least attractive of the two tyres this weekend. This was quite a bold move, but it paid off for both men, particularly Button. Ironically Sebastian Vettel, who had gone for an ultra-aggressive strategy with his first stop scheduled for lap 11, also selected the supersoft to start on, but his tyres went off very quickly and this slowed the field up behind him. This was a gift for the Brawn drivers as it gave them a cushion of more than 15 seconds over the chasing pack, including the two Ferraris and Nico Rosberg's Williams.

The key phase of the race as far as Button was concerned was the period towards the end of the first stint when Barrichello's supersoft tyres started to lose performance. His driving style is harder on the tyre than Button's and this gave Jenson a chance to build a big margin over his team-mate. During the second stint he achieved a 15-second cushion. Barrichello said afterwards that he had been forced to drive with loose seat belts, which made for an uncomfortable ride. He also said that the key to Button's win was the pole lap on Saturday. This was pretty much the only lap all weekend to that point where Jenson had been faster than Rubens, but it was the crucial one.

Button seems to have a knack for stepping up in the final lap in qualifying when the race fuel goes in and the new tyres are put on. He has more confidence in the car and in his own feel for the grip level. It's only fractional, but it's enough to swing it his way.

Make no mistake though, Rubens is helping him by pushing him very hard. He is also helping him on set up. As with his partnership with Michael Schumacher, Rubens is extremely good at dialling in a racing car and giving his team-mate cues on set up. It happened in Spain with Button and it happened again here. I'm sure this is one of the key reasons why Ross Brawn took Barrichello in preference to Bruno Senna or someone else. The choice has paid handsome dividends.

On Button's side, he will want an investigation into why he's had trouble dialling the car in the last two races, after seemingly no problems in that area in the first few events.

Ferrari have shown today that they are back in business and they will be in front of Brawn before too long. The next two races will favour Red Bull, with that car's liking for long fast corners. So Vettel and Webber will be in great shape. But Button is very comfortable now and can play the percentage game.

MONACO GRAND PRIX
Monaco 78 laps

1.	Button	Brawn GP-Mercedes	1h40:44.282
2.	Barrichello	Brawn GP-Mercedes	+ 7.666
3.	Raikkonen	Ferrari	+ 13.443
4.	Massa	Ferrari	+ 15.110
5.	Webber	Red Bull-Renault	+ 15.730
6.	Rosberg	Williams-Toyota	+ 33.586
7.	Alonso	Renault	+ 37.839
8.	Bourdais	Toro Rosso-Ferrari	+ 1:03.142

DRIVERS' STANDINGS

1. Button   51
2. Barrichello   35
3. Vettel   23
4. Webber   19.5
5. Trulli   14.5
6. Glock   12

CONSTRUCTORS' STANDINGS

1. Brawn GP-Mercedes   86
2. Red Bull-Renault   42.5
3. Toyota   26.5
4. Ferrari   17
5. McLaren-Mercedes   13
6. Renault   11

Toyota on way out of F1, BMW reflecting?
24 May 2009

This morning in Monaco there was plenty of discussion about the 2010 F1 rules and much speculation about what was going to happen next.

It seems to be becoming widely accepted that Toyota will use the situation to make its exit from Formula 1. They were thinking about this towards the end of 2008, but there seems to be a general belief among the other teams that they will go at the end of this year. BMW, which is having its worst season by far in F1, is also said to be reviewing its participation.

FIA president Max Mosley was making himself very available to the media and his message was that Ferrari will be staying in F1, "100% sure". But the sport will need to fill any empty grid slots and that is the area a lot of work is going into.

The word was that the teams and the FIA had kissed and made up and that everything was going to be sorted out by the 29 May deadline for entries, but team bosses I spoke to on the grid in Monaco sounded a note of caution. "Are you all loved up again?" I asked one, and he replied, "No, but we're falling in love again."

The teams say that they would like to start from the point of maintaining the 2009 regulations and go from there in terms of finding a consensus way of regulating the costs down to a level around the £40 million mark at which Max Mosley wants the budget cap set, perhaps by 2011. By then the world will be out of recession, in all probability, and new opportunities will be out there to generate income for the teams.

Mosley, who is still determined to maintain the idea of a budget cap, said, "I can imagine we can take it through one year if possible [with the] higher figure and then go to the full cap in 2011, but that's something under discussion. This is a possibility."

"Ultimately, it's going to have to be that sort of region," he said. "Just imagine in today's world, you go out to get sponsorship and you are just an ordinary team, so to raise 45 million euros is a massive undertaking.

"Everybody can talk figures, well it ought to be this figure or that figure, but if a team cannot raise the money, then there is nothing they can do."

Money is hard enough to find for the existing teams, look at the amount of sponsorship on the Brawn, and they have won five races!

It seems very hard to imagine new teams being able to raise the kind of money necessary to get into F1. But Mosley insists on new teams coming in, so discussions are concentrating on ways of helping new teams, with cheap engine and gearbox deals and a possible chassis-lease package to allow them to run competitively at low cost to start with. It seems that the existing teams are saying that they would require the new teams to run rookie drivers on that basis.

Why Williams had to look after itself
26 May 2009

I posted on Sunday morning that I had heard Williams were going to break ranks with the other Formula 1 teams and put in an entry for the 2010 season this week and they have done that.

I've been thinking about this, about why they have done it, what it will do to FOTA unity and where it leaves the other teams.

Williams have become the team closest to the FIA in recent times. In part this is due to a personal relationship between Williams CEO Adam Parr and Max Mosley. Both trained as barristers and I think they understand each other as a result. I also think Adam knows how to read Max pretty well.

On a more basic level Williams need to stay close to the FIA because all they do is race F1 cars, they don't sell energy drinks or road cars. So if they didn't put an entry in for 2010 what would they do with themselves and their 500-plus employees? They also stand to benefit from budgets coming down to £40 million. At that level they will not only be able to survive but to make a profit. And the technical department reckons that with many teams scaling down, they will do the best job at that level of investment.

Williams signed a contract back in 2005, shortly after Ferrari, to stay with the FIA and with FOM, rather than join the manufacturers' breakaway series being proposed at the time. The contract they signed then obliges them to race in F1 until the end of 2010. I don't know what time-frame is in the agreement Ferrari signed at that time, but Bernie Ecclestone referred to it the other day when he implied that he would sue them if they didn't enter next year.

The question now is, will the other teams who signed up in 2005 also be obliged to put an entry in for 2010? These teams are Red Bull, Toro Rosso and Force India (it was Midland at the time). It is unlikely that their deals are all the same as Williams's, because Ecclestone tends to like doing different deals with each participant.

For example, Frank Williams said on Friday that he knew Ferrari's deal paid them more money than Williams but he did not know that they had a right of veto over the rules.

It has been reported in the last couple of days that the other teams within FOTA are angry with Williams because they had signed a collective letter saying that they would not enter the championship. This isn't quite true. Williams refused to sign that letter, but they did sign a second, modified version, which did not commit them to collective action.

Judging from the noises coming out of Toyota at the moment, governance and transparency are their big bugbears, more than budget caps. Toyota and Ferrari have been working closely together at all levels and if Toyota are to leave the sport, I'm sure that they will say that it is because of the governance.

There is another meeting of FOTA this week, so the story will move on quite a bit before the entry deadline on Friday (29th).

* * *

The nine remaining teams in the Formula One Teams Association submitted a "conditional" entry for the 2010 world championship before the deadline.

Along with that single entry for all nine of them, they submitted a document with proposals for cost reduction to the FIA, which Toyota's John Howett describes as "comprehensive". There were two main conditions which they wanted to see fulfilled before their commitment could be confirmed. One was the signature of the Concorde Agreement by 12 June, the other was that the rules stay the same as 2009, i.e. no budget cap and no two-tier system.

Chapter Six
June 2009

June was the month when F1 took itself to the brink of the abyss and looked down deep inside it. Provoked by the uncompromising, hardline stance of FIA president Max Mosley, the teams decided to call Mosley's bluff and formed their own breakaway series. On the eve of the British Grand Prix they announced their decision.

The high stakes game of brinkmanship had reached its logical conclusion and a deal was soon sorted out, which also led to Mosley agreeing to stand down. Ultimately the whole thing was about egos: and Ferrari president Luca di Montezemolo was able to prove that Mosley's assertion in my Financial Times interview in May that F1 can survive without Ferrari was untrue.

Here in the blog entries from June you can retrace the steps that led the sport to the point of self-destruction and track the resolution of the teams to stay their course despite intense pressure on individuals from the FIA and Bernie Ecclestone.

* * *

Mosley: Let FOTA do their own series
3 June 2009

FIA president Max Mosley has broken his silence on the conditional entry the nine FOTA teams made last Friday to the 2010 world championship.

Speaking to Swiss paper *Motorsport Aktuell*, Mosley made it quite clear that he is not going to entertain FOTA's demands that the budget cap idea be abandoned, that the 2009 rules be carried over for next year and that the new Concorde Agreement be signed by 12 June, the date on which the successful entries will be announced.

"You cannot sign an agreement which was specified so late, before 12 June," he said, clearly unwilling to back down on the central point of his plan, which is the budget cap.

"I say, if you want to make the rules, then go and organise your own championship. Formula 1 is ours, we make the rules. We've started [like that] 60 years ago and we will continue like that."

Mosley wants new teams in F1 and believes that FOTA's conditional entry is a tactic. "It's quite clear that they want to slow down the process of application to the championship so that it will be too late for the new teams."

The FIA believe they have the FOTA teams exactly where they want them. They believe that Ferrari is subject to the same legally binding agreement to compete that has compelled Williams to enter and for that reason I think they will name Ferrari as an entrant on 12 June, despite the Italian team's desire to be part of the dissident group. After that it will be up to Ferrari to challenge for their right *not* to compete.

As for the rest, they may start to sweat a little as the date gets closer and they realise that when the music stops in this game of musical chairs, they might well be left with no chair. Mosley may have felt compelled to say something after almost a week of silence but he is not going to be the one blinking as things stand.

Button expects Red Bull onslaught
4 June 2009

Jenson Button sat down with the media this afternoon in Istanbul and as usual gave a well-considered analysis of where he stands in relation to the opposition. He feels that Red Bull are about to go on a bull run. The Englishman is clearly thinking a lot about all aspects of the rival teams, as is normal, but what is good is that he is prepared to share his thoughts with the media in a considered way.

"I think that the Red Bulls should work quite well here," he said. "The car that they had in Barcelona, if they brought that here they would be competitive. We'll have to see if their diffuser makes a difference on this circuit. But they're expected to be competitive and I think they will be.

"If you look at the times in the races previous to Monaco, they were very competitive. You could say that they have been as quick as us; they just haven't got it together over the race weekends.

"If you look through all the data of every race we've done their lap times are as competitive as us, certain teams, it's just that we've done a better job than them. They will get it right, just not too often hopefully."

Meanwhile Fernando Alonso said that he feels that Button is able to drive with something in hand, that he has not had to push at all times. According to Alonso the Brawn car has no weak points.

"It is the best car, there is no doubt. It's very good aerodynamically, it's very good mechanically, with good grip, because they can really attack the kerbs," he said. "They have a very strong car, they have finished all the races with both cars.

"They have very good starts, so there's no weak point at the moment. It's very difficult to beat them because it's difficult to find that weak point. They are the best in every area so that's quite impressive." He rather gloomily added that he thinks Button could wrap up the title by round 12 or 13.

What the teams mean to F1
6 June 2009

I wrote a piece on the ITV F1 website yesterday considering the prospects for the FOTA teams to start their own breakaway series, which they are being "encouraged" to do by FIA president Max Mosley.

I mentioned that Max always makes the point that the FIA owns F1 and if teams don't like it they can go and race elsewhere. The teams of course believe that they are the show.

Mosley compares the role of teams in F1 to customers in a restaurant; they may eat there every day and spend a great deal of money doing so, but that doesn't mean they own the restaurant. Well, overnight I received this message, I won't say who it's from, but I thought I would share it with you:

"When you eat in a restaurant, you don't have to buy the food, bring the food, create the recipes, bring the chefs, bring the waiters, and cook it and serve it to yourself, do you?

"Whereas, in Formula 1, the teams do indeed do the equivalent of that (i.e. pay for the factories in which the cars are built, hire and pay the workers who design and build them, hire and pay the drivers who drive them, hire and pay the guys who run them at races, hire and pay the guys who find the sponsors, who in turn help pay for it all, etc etc).

"A more accurate analogy of what the FIA provides would be an empty room in which one was allowed to provide the kitchen equipment and the staff, at one's own expense, and then cook and serve the meal to oneself."

There is of course another dimension to this whole dispute, which is the television coverage. No one televises you eating in a restaurant, but the F1 teams put on a spectacular show, which raises around £800 million a year in revenues from television companies, of which the teams receive 50 per cent. That is where the key to this lies. What exactly is the show, is it the restaurant itself or is it the quality of the feast the teams serve up?

Button puts Red Bull in their place
7 June 2009

Jenson Button won the Turkish Grand Prix today, by 6.7 seconds over the Red Bull duo of Mark Webber and pole sitter Sebastian Vettel. It was Button's sixth win from seven starts and sets him up now for the world championship and an emotional homecoming to Silverstone in two weeks time.

"You have built me a monster of a car," he told the team over the radio afterwards. He later added, "The car felt the best it has felt all year."

It was a dominant performance by Button, who started second on the grid, but passed Vettel on the opening lap when the German made a mistake and ran wide, letting Button through.

After that Red Bull tried to recover the situation by putting Vettel on a three-stop strategy which called for him to attack Button who was heavier on a two stopper. Vettel caught him, but could not pass. After that he lost time with the result that Webber leapfrogged him at the second stops to take second place.

Vettel was pretty disgruntled about it, "I'm not happy, " he said, adding that after his mistake on the opening lap he expected the team would switch him to a two stop strategy like Webber's. This didn't happen. He has lost ground not only to Button but also to team mate Webber, who is now just 2.5 points behind in the championship. The two had gone different routes on strategy, but it's important to remember that Vettel and Webber set an almost identical lap time in qualifying, when fuel loads are taken into account.

Rubens Barrichello in the other Brawn car had a poor start, which dropped him to P13, he later retired from the race, Brawn's first retirement of the season.

The race saw a return to form for Toyota, with Jarno Trulli in fourth place after a dire time in Monaco and for Williams for whom Rosberg was 5th.

But the Ferraris disappointed. Massa finished 6th, half a minute behind the winner, with Raikkonen 9th.

BMW Sauber were back in the points, with Robert Kubica in seventh place thanks to a new double diffuser and other updates to their car.

TURKISH GRAND PRIX
Istanbul 58 laps

1.	Button	Brawn GP-Mercedes	1h26:24.848
2.	Webber	Red Bull-Renault	+ 6.714
3.	Vettel	Red Bull-Renault	+ 7.461
4.	Trulli	Toyota	+ 27.843
5.	Rosberg	Williams-Toyota	+ 31.539
6.	Massa	Ferrari	+ 39.996
7.	Kubica	BMW Sauber	+ 46.247
8.	Glock	Toyota	+ 46.959

DRIVERS' STANDINGS
1. Button 61
2. Barrichello 35
3. Vettel 29
4. Webber 27.5
5. Trulli 19.5
6. Glock 13

CONSTRUCTORS' STANDINGS
1. Brawn GP-Mercedes 96
2. Red Bull-Renault 56.5
3. Toyota 32.5
4. Ferrari 20
5. McLaren-Mercedes 13
6. Williams-Toyota 11.5

Williams and Brawn: two perspectives on a crisis
8 June 2009

"Williams needs a budget cap. Hopefully it will bring the others down to us." Such was the view of Sir Frank Williams on Saturday afternoon, discussing the ongoing crisis over the 2010 rules.

Frank has signed up for the FIA championship next season. After years of almost bankrupting itself to stay competitive in F1, the Williams team welcomes the budget cap as an opportunity to take a financial breather, make the team profitable again and shape it up for a possible sale down the line. Frank is also attracted by the idea of housing one of the new teams on his factory site, so he could offset some costs and make the budget cap work better for him.

Also being quite vocal over the weekend, but from the opposite angle, was Ross Brawn, who still sides with the FOTA teams. FOTA is only prepared to enter next year if two important conditions are met, one of which is that the 2009 rules remain until a new set of rules can be agreed through what FOTA considers to be the proper rule-making channels.

On the face of it, Ross and Frank are in the same boat; their teams both exist only to race in F1, they are both independents and therefore reliant on manufacturers for their engine supply. But Frank has sided with the FIA because of a legally binding agreement to race in F1 until 2012 (as previously noted, the FIA contends that Ferrari has a similar contract in place), while Ross believes his best interests are served by staying with FOTA.

Here's Frank: "Ferrari is a key point. The curious thing is that Ferrari is not part of the FIA camp. I don't think anyone is going to die about this. Max doesn't want this to turn to poo, spread all over the papers for the next six months, what damage [people] did to F1. I think there is a will to say 'Let's be human for a change and talk to each other'.

"Max isn't looking for a fight, he just wants to avoid having teams leave, smaller ones in particular because they cannot afford to continue."

Frank also said that he feels that Bernie Ecclestone could really do without this turning into a civil war because he's getting on a bit in years (he turns 79 in September) and doesn't have the energy for such a fight.

Ross Brawn comes at this from a different point of view, mindful of the fact that his team wouldn't be on the grid this year were it not for the support that they received from the other teams over the winter.

"The existence of this team was dependent on the support of FOTA teams - McLaren and Mercedes in particular are the reason why we are here, and I think the FOTA initiatives are good. We seem to have had a disconnection in terms of liaising and negotiating with the FIA, and that has perhaps been the problem because FOTA has got a lot of good ideas and the FIA has got a lot of good ideas. Hopefully those ideas will be brought together to find a solution.

"I think there are interim solutions, but quite clearly if next Friday 10 [new] teams are given an entry in F1, then there is a problem because there is no room for the rest of us. And I don't know what will happen then. Even if it is a holding position until we sort this out, I hope we can find a solution."

The manufacturers are all bound to each other with a €50 million forfeit if one of them jumps ship, but the pressure on Brawn to split from them is intense, especially as the current championship leader. From what he has been saying recently, that isn't going to happen.

Bernie says "It's my show" - Renault boss disagrees
11 June 2009

There are two contrasting quotes in the press today. The first comes from Bernie Ecclestone, highlighting what he brings to F1 and why it is the show that it is, while the president of Renault, Carlos Ghosn, has come out and expressed the view "that the teams should take back control of Formula 1".

Bernie, speaking to the *Daily Express*, said, "It costs a lot of money to set up a series. Right now, we supply the venues at no cost to the teams, they roll up with all their sponsors' names and money and race in front of a huge television audience which I supply through the contracts we win.

"That money flows back to the teams and they spend it. It would be different when they have to provide all the venues, hire their own race people, find their own television companies – and we have the best – and promote it."

Meanwhile Ghosn has made his feelings very clear too, according to a quote given by news agency AFP. "We are the ones doing the show, who bring in the technology, who bring in the engines, who hire the drivers. And if we do the show, the revenues of Formula 1 must come back to us. Today we pay to be in Formula 1; that is not normal. Intermediaries have made enough money with this. We want to take back control of Formula 1."

Representatives of FOTA met yesterday in London to finalise their approach to FIA president Max Mosley at a meeting due to take place in London this morning. Three of the team bosses have been detailed to attend the meeting, Ferrari's Stefano Domenicali, Red Bull's Christian Horner and Toyota's John Howett.

FIA enters Ferrari in 2010 World Championship
12 June 2009

After all the talk, the speculation and the drama, the FIA published the 2010 entry list shortly after 10am today.

The key point is that the FIA has gone ahead and listed all five of the teams who signed up in 2005 as unconditionally entered into the world championship, including Ferrari, which it has placed top of the list. This is likely to provoke a strong reaction from Italy.

Williams and Force India had already entered, but the two Red Bull teams join Ferrari on the list of forced entrants despite being part of the FOTA conditional entry group, who wanted to see major changes to the rules *before* making their entry official.

Ferrari will have little choice now but to mount a legal challenge to the validity of the contract, which means a test case in court.

Of the many new teams who made an entry only three have been accepted, Peter Windsor's USF1, Campos and Manor Motorsport, whom no one has been talking about. Manor have been immensely successful in categories up to Formula 3 and Lewis Hamilton once drove for them in Formula Renault, but they are a long way off F1.

Cosworth is back on the grid, with all three of the new teams signed up for their engines. There is some suggestion that USF1 are thinking about switching to a Toyota engine.

Prodrive is not there, but a note at the bottom of the list suggests that other new teams may be given an entry if negotiations with FOTA due to take place before 19 June should fail. It is also believed that there are some reserve teams should any of the manufacturers take this opportunity to quit the sport, Toyota, BMW and Renault being the ones whose participation is still in doubt in F1 circles. The FIA World Council will meet a few days later to ratify everything.

Also of note is the fact that Red Bull, Toro Rosso and Brawn have no engine deal for 2010 in place at this time.

* * *

Ferrari's response was swift and decisive. "Despite Ferrari's previous written notice to the FIA not to do so, the FIA has included Ferrari as an unconditional participant in next year's Formula One World Championship", a statement said.

"For the avoidance of any doubt, Ferrari reaffirms that it shall not take part in the 2010 FIA Formula One World Championship under the regulations adopted by the FIA in violation of Ferrari's rights under a written agreement with the FIA."

A few days later the European Automobile Manufacturers' Association got involved, issuing a statement which said, "Today, the members of the Board of the European Automobile Manufacturer's Association discussed the current situation prevailing in Formula 1, and have concluded that the current govern-ance system cannot continue."

This stance represented an open challenge to Mosley's leadership and the architect of it was Renault's Carlos Ghosn. Later in the year there would be some payback from this for Renault.

* * *

How the new F1 teams were chosen
12 June 2009

"With the financial reforms to lower the barrier to entry to realistic levels it is good to see such a strong market for new teams," said the FIA this afternoon in a second official statement, following on from the announcement that F1 will have three new teams on the grid next season. "This exercise has demonstrated that the only reason there have been vacancies on the F1 grid for many years was the excessive cost of participation."

This is what the FIA has maintained all along was its main motivation for introducing dramatic cost reductions and even the budget cap. Judging from the extensive comments on this site over recent weeks, it seems that a lot of people welcome the idea of fresh blood in F1, provided it is stable and has a strong chance of surviving more than a few months in the bear-pit of F1.

The FIA revealed that there were 15 applications for the championship from new teams, some of whom were chancers, others deadly serious. From the chatter I've heard in racing circles, they have unsurprisingly picked the ones who have got their ducks in a line, namely Campos and USF1, the only slight surprises for me are the absence of Prodrive and the inclusion of Manor Motorsport, who will operate in partnership with Nick Wirth, formerly with Simtek and Benetton. Each team went through a due diligence process overseen by the FIA's Tony Purnell, the ex-Jaguar F1 boss who has been advising Max Mosley.

The primary concern, obviously, was to ensure that adequate funding was in place. USF1 has raised around $60 million of start-up capital from US investors in Silicon Valley. There are rumours that one of the founders of You Tube has put money in.

Adrian Campos has always been very good at raising money in his GP2 ventures and he has run a successful team. The team, now called Barwa, is leading the GP2 championship at the moment with Romain Grosjean at the wheel. Campos is also the man who discovered Fernando Alonso, so his credentials are pretty respectable.

So how did the due diligence process work? "Once we had formed an opinion of the serious contenders we asked them to come to London to be questioned face-to-face by the due diligence team. Then a short summary report on the top five was sent to the FIA President. The process was conducted with the professional assistance of Deloitte."

Prodrive boss David Richards was surprised and probably rather embarrassed not to have had his entry accepted. Of all the proposed entrants he is the one with the most senior F1 experience and his company has succeeded at the highest levels of motorsport in sports cars and rallying. He also has wealthy backers from the Middle East.

* * *

Richards later claimed that the only reason his entry was not accepted was because only teams using Cosworth engines were taken on and his business model had always been based around a deal with Mercedes. Other teams complained about the selection process and threatened to take the matter to the European courts.

* * *

Teams attack chief F1 steward's impartiality
14 June 2009

There is a story in the Italian newspaper *Corriere della Sera* today about a letter sent by the FOTA teams yesterday (Saturday 13 June) to the FIA complaining about the behaviour of the FIA's Alan Donnelly at the recent Turkish Grand Prix. The letter alleges that Donnelly was going around from team to team telling them to abandon the FOTA stance and sign up for 2010. The teams did not consider this appropriate behaviour for a man whose role at the races is to convene and oversee the stewards and to take a totally impartial view of problems arising on the track.

The teams have requested Mosley's comment on the matter.

Hamilton buries the hatchet and the throttle
14 June 2009

I was lucky enough to be at Silverstone last Wednesday, to spend the day with McLaren, driving the 650 bhp Mercedes SLR and being driven in it by the reigning world champion.

This was part of the Lewis Hamilton-British media rehabilitation exercise, particularly targeted at the Fleet Street guys after things got a bit out of control post the Melbourne-lying-to-stewards business.

Hamilton got pretty wound up by some of the coverage and initially tried a policy of non co-operation, but recently he has changed tack and this day at Silverstone was a way of hitting the reset button. He spent most of the day there and was very affable, even to some journalists he'd been monosyllabic with a month ago.

It's all a giant game, with the press, and you just have to accept that and learn how to play it. Nigel Mansell found the same and Damon Hill too. The advantage they had was that they were far more mature than Hamilton at the time they had to deal with it and also they had each had a life before becoming famous. Hamilton has had a lot to come to terms with this year; an uncompetitive car as well as question-marks against his integrity, so troubles with the press are perhaps the easiest of his problems to fix.

Damon Hill was there too on Wednesday and made the astute observation that for a British driver at the British Grand Prix, it is difficult not being competitive at Silverstone.

Hamilton wowed the journos with his sublime car control on a miserably wet day. I went first because they did it alphabetically and so it was a voyage of discovery as much for the driver as it was for the passenger on the shiny wet track. I can honestly say that the car was rarely pointing straight, apart from on the Hangar Straight. The rest of the time it was fishtailing around, as we hit the standing water at tremendous speed.

Afterwards we were offered a cup of tea and a scone (yes, really) in the BRDC clubhouse and Lewis gave us his views on what it will be like racing at his home Grand Prix with no chance of winning. How tough is it, he was asked, to accept not being competitive?

"I think I've always known how to deal with it all but it's about knowing how to accept it. I won't accept that the car is not quick enough, keep pushing, keep pushing, but then you have to accept that this is probably around the place you are gong to finish. But you keep pushing and keep your mind in a certain readiness for the potential to win. It makes you stronger, it's not all about running at the front."

F1 power struggle coming to a head
17 June 2009

I have a feeling that the end is in sight in the battle between the FIA and FOTA. I've spent the day on the phone to many of the interested parties and read the statements issued by the FIA. It looks like Friday will be put-up or shut-up day.

The first statement this morning was about the negotiations over how budget restrictions are controlled, and stated that the negotiations were now over: the budget cap stays.

Later the FIA put out a long document recounting the history, as they see it, of the whole process and of FOTA's conduct during it. The document went on to suggest that FOTA wanted to take over the F1 world championship,

"In light of the success of the FIA's Championship, FOTA – made up of participants who come and go as it suits them – has set itself two clear objectives: to take over the regulation of Formula One from the FIA and to expropriate the commercial rights for itself. These are not objectives which the FIA can accept."

Ferrari argue that they have created the history, but this sentence isn't aimed at them. A bit further on this memorable line appears, "Good governance does not mean that Ferrari should govern." As a sentence it is almost Obama-esque in its balance, but the meaning is one-sided.

It seems clear now that the talking has stopped. The time is fast approaching for the five teams, whose entry is conditional, to either enter the championship or go off and start their own series. Of those five, Brawn GP and McLaren are under the most pressure. Surely they will have to think very seriously about the wisdom of not entering, while the other three manufacturer teams, Toyota, Renault and BMW would have to either do a dramatic U-turn or leave the sport. Many people in F1 circles believe that this is Mosley's agenda. If that were to happen then there would be spaces for Prodrive and two other new teams.

The alternative for the five teams would be to form a breakaway group and hope that Ferrari won its legal battle with the FIA and FOM. That could take months to resolve though, and it would be hard to plan a breakaway without knowing that Ferrari was definitely part of it.

The FIA believes it has Ferrari, Red Bull and Toro Rosso under contract, the same contract as it has Force India and Williams under. I've spoken to Williams's Adam Parr, a barrister, about this and in his view the contract is watertight, which is why they have entered. Ferrari says it isn't, because the FIA breached it when drawing up the 2010 rules.

Red Bull and Toro Rosso have stayed in the FOTA camp this long so as to be able to see the whole picture and have put their name to every letter and statement. But Red Bull boss Dietrich Mateschitz has always been close to Mosley and, despite protestations from the Red Bull team, I wonder whether they will sign up on Friday, as racing is all those two teams exist for.

The end is nigh... as those men with the sandwich boards are wont to warn us, and it looks like F1 is heading for the worst outcome.

* * *

The teams wanted the FIA to consider dropping the idea of an enforced budget cap and replacing it with a "resource restriction" agreement between teams. For many teams, especially Ferrari, the idea of having FIA auditors crawling all over their books was intolerable. Mosley wanted the budget cap and refused to budge on this. But ultimately the teams got their way.

* * *

Mosley versus FOTA - is there any talking to be done?
18 June 2009

A tense day ahead at Silverstone for everybody. The teams proposed that tomorrow's deadline be moved on to 1 July, to allow more time for discussion, but that was rebuffed by FIA president Max Mosley yesterday. The FOTA teams also sent a letter to Mosley with suggestions for a compromise to the issue of budget caps, and the method of financial control.

> "We detect... that a solution might be possible based on the FOTA resource restriction proposal but with measures introduced," the letter said.

> "We would propose in this respect that we nominate a top firm of independent accountants who will devise an audit methodology that will be implemented by all of the teams."

Later in the day Mosley wrote back in a letter which was widely circulated, with his version of the compromise he would be prepared to accept. Once again this was based on the teams all signing up unconditionally and then negotiating changes to the rules from within. Mosley has said repeatedly that there has to be a cap. He has offered for a mutually acceptable auditor to be the investigator should policing be required.

Mosley confirmed that there would be no two-tier system of rules, but that Cosworth, which has not built a new F1 engine for three years, would be allowed to run their engine unrestricted.

A letter will go out today or tomorrow in Silverstone requesting signatures from all the FOTA teams by the deadline of Friday.

With their actions last week, the teams have got themselves into a position where they seem to be suggesting that a deal can only be done if Mosley doesn't stay in his role and steps down. Mosley, for his part, is sticking to his guns.

Who will blink first?

I got a message that day from one of my readers, Charlie. It put a smile on my face, in what was becoming a very tense situation,

"James, Do you remember me taking your advice and putting £20 on Brawn to win the Championship? at 15-1? well I got an email from Paddypower this morning saying that they've decided to accept reality and settle all bets on Jenson Button to win the World Drivers Championship and Brawn to win the World Constructors Championship as winners, four months before the end of the season!"

* * *

FOTA goes for breakaway, F1 holds its breath
19 June 2009

"If you are going to bark, you need to be prepared to bite." This is what a member of one of the FOTA teams said to me yesterday afternoon.

Shortly after midnight FOTA made the announcement that many had feared was coming and which takes the sport into uncharted waters. The teams met at the Renault HQ near Oxford prior to making their announcement:

> "(The) teams have no alternative other than to commence the preparation for a new championship which reflects the values of its participants and partners. This series will have transparent governance, one set of regulations, encourage more entrants and listen to the wishes of the fans, including offering lower prices for spectators worldwide, partners and other important stakeholders. The major drivers, stars, brands, sponsors, promoters and companies historically associated with the highest level of motorsport will all feature in this new series."

Of course commencing preparation for a new series is not the same as closing the door on F1 and walking away. The teams expect a compromise to be found and are trying to force it. It has always been the case that if they stay together they can achieve something, but if they allow themselves to be split they will fail. So they have gone for it and put the ball back in the FIA and Bernie Ecclestone's court.

This is going to cause damage to F1 whatever happens. There could be a swift resolution through negotiation, for after all the gap between the two sides is not that great and both want to achieve the same things. The split has been caused by different ideologies and increasingly the FOTA teams have come to resent and be angered by the way in which the FIA has governed in this situation.

Today is the FIA's deadline for finding a solution and FOTA have pre-empted events by issuing their statement during the night, allowing a day of frantic diplomacy to take place. It is going to be one of those very dramatic days in the paddock.

The television executives will be really alarmed. They see the numbers on F1, understand the commercial proposition and sign off cheques for tens of millions of pounds a year. But many of them do not understand the sport itself and will be unhappy with the prospect of holding the rights to a series which on the face of it consists of Williams, Force India and some new teams. Circuit owners and regional governments will feel the same way. And it will not make it any easier for Donington to find investment, either.

Of course the FIA is confident that it has a binding contract with Ferrari to race in F1 and if the rift continues that contract will have to be tested in a court of law.

The statement continues:

> "FOTA is proud that it has achieved the most substantial measures to reduce costs in the history of our sport. In particular the manufacturer teams have provided assistance to the independent teams, a number of which would probably not be in the sport today without the FOTA initiatives. The FOTA teams have further agreed upon a substantial voluntary cost reduction that provides a sustainable model for the future.

> "Following these efforts all the teams have confirmed to the FIA and the commercial rights holder that they are willing to commit until the end of 2012. The FIA and the commercial

rights holder have campaigned to divide FOTA. The wishes of the majority of the teams are ignored.

"Furthermore, tens of millions of dollars have been withheld from many teams by the commercial rights holder, going back as far as 2006. Despite this and the uncompromising environment, FOTA has genuinely sought compromise. It has become clear however, that the teams cannot continue to compromise on the fundamental values of the sport and have declined to alter their original conditional entries to the 2010 world championship. "

A lot of the focus will now fall on Bernie Ecclestone, the 78-year-old chief executive of the body which holds the commercial rights to the sport. He threatened a hailstorm of writs if the teams took this step. His reaction and that of the FIA will be interesting. They have pushed FOTA to this point, apparently to see what would happen. But did they really think that it would come to this?

* * *

That afternoon the FIA put out a statement saying that they were preparing legal action: "The FIA's lawyers have now examined the FOTA threat to begin a breakaway series. The actions of FOTA as a whole, and Ferrari in particular, amount to serious violations of law including wilful interference with contractual relations, direct breaches of Ferrari's legal obligations and a grave violation of competition law. The FIA will be issuing legal proceedings without delay."

* * *

Race day at Silverstone
21 June 2009

There is a fantastic atmosphere here at Silverstone today, with over 100,000 people looking forward to a great day's racing. We had 85,000 here on Friday, which is more than most Grands Prix get on race-day.

Bernie Ecclestone's comments yesterday that we will be back at Silverstone next year if Donington isn't ready have been well received by the F1 fraternity and the public and it has given some reassurance in a weekend of instability.

The weather is not as warm as predicted, it's currently only 15 degrees, which is not going to help Jenson Button very much. He needs the track to be warmer to get the tyres working properly on his Brawn Mercedes car. The crowd knows that Button is up against it today. Vettel and Red Bull are in such a strong position.

The paddock is abuzz, as it has been all weekend. Mid-morning, Max Mosley arrived in a Mercedes van with Bernie Ecclestone. Notwithstanding Max calling the FOTA breakaway members "loonies", the pair have been engaged in a lot of behind the scenes dialogue with the teams to try to find a solution.

Mosley is convinced that Flavio Briatore wants to become the Bernie of the new series. Time will tell. The dispute is probably not going to be resolved quickly, although the sponsors and TV companies desperately want it to be. I notice that the Director General of the BBC, Mark Thompson, is here today too, casting an eye over his corporation's huge investment. He looked edgy.

Personally I still believe that the key to it all is Ferrari's contract with the FIA and FOM. That is being looked at in a civil court in Switzerland at the moment. If the court decides that Ferrari are free agents then a deal will surely be done.

FOTA is serious about a breakaway, but they would prefer to race in F1 provided the circumstances were right.

Vettel crushes the opposition at Silverstone
21 June 2009

Sebastian Vettel put in a peerless performance today to win the British Grand Prix, his second victory of the season and the third of his brief career. He turns 22 next week.

Red Bull Racing have made big improvements to their car, but there is no doubt that the circuit and the conditions played to their strengths and Brawn's weaknesses as well. The Brawn drivers were struggling, relatively speaking. Button had a tougher time than Barrichello, but it was interesting that none of the other cars was fast enough to beat the Brawn to the podium. The question now is whether or not Red Bull will be ahead in the second half of the season and make a championship of it. They were faster in Istanbul, but Vettel made a mistake on the opening lap.

Webber was unlucky this weekend. He looked to have the measure of Vettel in the run up to qualifying - there was nothing in it. Red Bull gave Webber the lighter fuel load for qualifying which meant he was supposed to get the pole, but Vettel was given the better race strategy. The team was meticulously fair with the drivers, who were told that they could race each other. Some people are suggesting that Vettel should now be given the best of everything as he has closed the gap on Button to 23 points, which is the kind of gap Kimi Raikkonen was able to close up on Lewis Hamilton in 2007.

So will Webber be the number two from now on? Given that he is only 4.5 points behind Vettel that would be harsh. It certainly looks as if the Red Bull drivers will close the gap on Button, but whether they can really make a championship of it we will know after the next two races.

Ferrari and Williams both had good days. Ferrari took Felipe Massa from 11th on the grid to fourth, while Williams converted a good qualifying performance by both cars into a solid four points for Nico Rosberg in fifth place. Their respective team-mates both had days which started promisingly but ended in disappointment, Raikkonen running fifth in the early stages but finishing eighth and Nakajima a very positive fourth in the opening stint, but his early stop pit strategy dropped him down to 11th.

BRITISH GRAND PRIX
Silverstone 60 laps

1. Vettel	Red Bull-Renault		1h22:49.328
2. Webber	Red Bull-Renault	+	15.188
3. Barrichello	Brawn GP-Mercedes	+	41.175
4. Massa	Ferrari	+	45.043
5. Rosberg	Williams-Toyota	+	45.915
6. Button	Brawn GP-Mercedes	+	46.285
7. Trulli	Toyota	+	1:08.307
8. Raikkonen	Ferrari	+	1:09.622

DRIVERS' STANDINGS
1. Button   64
2. Barrichello   41
3. Vettel   39
4. Webber   35.5
5. Trulli   21.5
6. Massa   16

CONSTRUCTORS' STANDINGS
1. Brawn GP-Mercedes   105
2. Red Bull-Renault   74.5
3. Toyota   34.5
4. Ferrari   26
5. Williams-Toyota   15.5
6. McLaren-Mercedes   13

1

2 **3**

1 › Fernando Alonso's move to Ferrari was first tipped in December 2008, it was the big rumour of the season and was confirmed in September

2 › Felipe Massa had an horrific accident in Budapest, but was back in a car two months later and will race again in 2010

3 › The iconic Prancing Horse of **Ferrari**, the team which F1 learned in 2009 that it cannot do without

4 **5**

6 **7**

4 › Sebastian Vettel came of age as a driver in 2009, winning four races for Red Bull

5 › F1 almost destroyed itself in 2009, but it remains the most colourful and attractive of sports

6 › It was a tough start to the year for **Hamilton**, and his image took a knock, but he bounced back and won races

7 › Ross Brawn staked his claim to be considered one of the greatest engineers in F1 history after winning with his own team as well as Ferrari

8   9

8 › F1 drivers model
clothes designed by
Bernie Ecclestone's
daughter Petra.
Drivers still
epitomise glamour

9 › Nelson Piquet
refused to take his
sacking by Renault
lying down and
unleashed the
Singapore crash
fixing scandal

10

11

12

10 › Max Mosley's
vision of how F1
should tackle
the credit crunch
differed from
the teams' and
it triggered a
power struggle

11 › Flavio Briatore
was banned for life
by the FIA for his
part in the plot to
fix the Singapore
Grand Prix, a
judgement he
fought in court

**12 › Bernie
Ecclestone** had a
difficult year with
a divorce, a threat
to his empire from
the teams and a
furore over his
praise for Hitler

13

13 › In a complete
reversal of the
previous year's
form **Jenson Button**
won six of the first
seven races

Briatore makes the running in breakaway F1 series
22 June 2009

The indications coming from the FOTA teams on Sunday evening were quite resolute. They are not swayed by the latest suggestions from Max Mosley of fresh dialogue and are pressing ahead with their preparations for a breakaway series. Currently Flavio Briatore is making the running on this. Given his strong reputation as a wheeler-dealer, he is being positioned as the new Bernie in the FOTA set up, as we all suspected. He has been in touch with several of the F1 circuits, sounding them out, preparing the ground. (Several circuits are under the control of the teams anyway, like Fuji (Toyota) and Mugello (Ferrari).)

"We will have it ready in the next few weeks. We have been planning for several weeks already. We want a Formula One championship organised by FOTA, " said Briatore.

The Italian is a credible figure in this role. He and FOTA will appoint agents to start discussions with the television companies. I would imagine they will insist on free-to-air, rather than pay companies such as Sky, but we will see. It's going to be tough in this climate. In the UK, neither ITV, Channel 4 nor Channel 5 would have much money to offer for a breakaway series, especially as most television executives would know from experience that divided sports championships don't usually work. Common sense tells you that everyone would prefer to retain a Formula 1 world championship with all the strong teams in it. FOTA's viewpoint is that if they have to create their own series, then they will.

We are in a phoney war period now. There will be claims, counter-claims and rumours swirling around as each side looks to exploit the other's weak points. For example, there were rumours yesterday of Mosley dropping the legal action against FOTA , which came out of an interview he did on Sky Italia. (Ferrari is certainly not dropping its arbitration claim against the FIA in Lausanne, which started last Monday.)

The deal which saved F1
24 June 2009

The threatened breakaway is over! Formula 1 looked into the abyss, didn't like what it saw and has stepped away from the brink today as a deal has been struck. The FOTA teams will commit to race in the FIA F1 World Championship and Max Mosley has agreed to step down as FIA president from October.

The commitment from the manufacturers and teams appears to be only until 2012, not the 2014 commitment that Bernie Ecclestone and Max Mosley were looking for. The FIA has issued the entry list for next season's F1 world championship and it features all of the existing teams plus the three new ones who entered last week.

The deal was brokered by Luca di Montezemolo, Max Mosley and Bernie Ecclestone in Paris. In addition to the points mentioned above, the rules for next year will be the same as for 2009 and costs will be brought right down, but there will be no budget cap. Instead teams will act together to drastically reduce costs, down to a level of around £40 million in two years time.

The FIA emerges from the episode with its authority intact and a more sensible attitude from the teams to spending, FOTA emerges as a strong body which achieved a lot through staying united and Bernie Ecclestone and his partners, CVC, know that the cashflows will continue for at least another three years.

The rules may be as they were in 2009, but this is really only a starting point. The devil will be in the detail; will they go ahead with the ban on refuelling, for example? Will there be KERS? There is still more work to be done on this and FOTA meets tomorrow at noon, to move forward on finalising things in conjunction with the FIA.

The teams and manufacturers may have agreed to commit to 2012, but the deals with the FIA and FOM are different. This is a key point for FOTA. The FIA deal is open-ended, recognising the FIA's right to be the regulator of the sport, but now with the F1 Commission in place to decide on future rules, which was not the case recently. With regard to FOM, the teams are signed up until 2012, presumably on the same commercial terms, but they have separated their dealings with FOM from their dealings with the FIA.

Max Mosley will not seek re-election in October when his current term expires. In the meantime he has relinquished his position as the main contact man at the FIA for F1. Instead the FIA senate will deal with any issues in F1. Mosley is a member of the senate and, under FIA rules, he will remain a member in future as an ex-president. There is a sense here that if this deal were to fall through then Mosley would be on hand to take up the FIA's side again. Meanwhile there will be an election for a new FIA president in due course.

Both sides have therefore achieved much of what they wanted. By pushing the teams right over the brink, Mosley has got new teams into the sport, forced the manufacturers to commit and got them and the teams to wake up and smell the coffee when it comes to budgets.

So what provided the breakthrough? Well on the FIA's side it was FOTA's acknowledgement of the FIA's authority, their right to govern and regulate F1. On FOTA's side it was Mosley's agreement not to stand again and the return of the F1 Commission for setting new rules.

FOTA has achieved a lot and will no doubt continue as the body which represents the teams and manufacturers in dealings with the FIA and FOM in future. I imagine that Williams and Force India will be readmitted to FOTA, having sat on the sidelines throughout this latest process.

Leaving their respective methods to one side, to me this episode shows that Mosley has always been a long-term thinker, whereas the teams are more short-term. It has been a painful and protracted dispute and it's not completely over yet, but the sport should emerge the stronger from it.

* * *

But the story didn't end at this point; there was a twist. FOTA and Ferrari president Luca di Montezemolo made a tactical error by "dancing on Mosley's grave" somewhat prematurely. The triumphal tone of his press briefing offended Mosley and opened up a fresh rift.

"The satisfaction is that all of our requests have been accepted", said Montezemolo. "To us, three things were most important; that F1 stay F1 and not become F3,

that there is no dictator, but that there was a choice of rules, agreed and not imposed; and that whoever had a team was consulted and had a voice. Mosley has announced that in October he will stand down, with an irrevocable decision, and that from now on he won't get involved in F1."

Mosley responded angrily, "Given your and FOTA's deliberate attempt to mislead the media, I now consider my options open. At least until October, I am president of the FIA with the full authority of that office."

* * *

Playing the F1 media game
29 June 2009

With a three-week gap between Silverstone and Nürburgring, a one-sided championship and not much other news around, the Max Mosley versus FOTA story is taking up most of the space at the moment.

Yesterday in the *Mail on Sunday* Mosley gave a long interview with veteran journo Malcolm Folley all about how FOTA had danced on his grave somewhat prematurely. I posted on Thursday that I found the triumphal tone of the response from FOTA to the peace deal rather surprising and it seems that Mosley and the FIA members took it badly, to the extent, according to the *MoS* interview, that the FIA membership is spoiling for a fight with FOTA and in particular with the car-makers.

Mosley signs off the interview, "I do not want to leave the president's office in a way where it was suggested that people from the car industry had pushed me out. If that impression is not completely dispelled, the clubs are going to insist that I stand again. So I hope very much that it will be dispelled before we get to that point."

I don't think Mosley wants to stand again; he would rather hand the reins over to Jean Todt and take more of a background role, but for the moment the impression he wants to create is that he might be asked to continue by those supporters who feel that the FIA is under threat. He has said this kind of thing before and he has always been duly re-elected.

What is fascinating is that this dialogue has been conducted almost entirely through the media, either via interviews, press conferences, press releases or leaked letters. There has been a plethora of informa-tion for the media, but for the public as well.

FOTA was a little slow to cotton on to this technique, or perhaps they didn't want to adopt it themselves at the beginning, but have come round to it now by engaging the services of PR company New Century shortly before the Silverstone showdown.

The deal to save F1 itself may have been hammered out behind closed doors, but not much else has been. Mosley has certainly shifted his approach to these battles. One is tempted to say that since his run-in with the *News of the World* last year, he has realised how to harness the full power of the modern media, including the 24-hour news cycle and the online world, to affect the trajectory of a negotiation.

Because FOTA too has evolved into a different beast from the disparate bunch of F1 teams with conflicting interests we had before, Mosley has developed a different method for taking them on. He has shown that a group with so many manufacturers at the heart of it cannot deal with bad headlines as easily as he himself can.

Mosley has used insinuation a lot, for example in the most recent letter, where he wrote about a certain team, which had attempted to influence the path of the appeal court hearing into the double diffusers to get them banned. He does not name the team, but leads people to infer that it might be Ferrari, based on previous experience, but then again it might not be, it might be Red Bull or McLaren or Renault. This kind of tactic infuriated FOTA.

Today there is calm again as everyone takes stock. FOTA still seem not to be too worried by this latest twist, but Mosley has four more months in office in which a great deal can happen.

A chat with Richard Cregan about Abu Dhabi
30 June 2009

The new Yas Marina Island circuit at Abu Dhabi is taking shape, ahead of its first Grand Prix on 1 November, the season finale. Today the organisers launched a video game, which offers fans the chance to drive a virtual lap of the circuit.

At Silverstone I sat down for a few minutes' chat with Richard Cregan, who is CEO of the project and responsible for bringing it in on time and to the highest F1 standards. We met in the new Ferrari motorhome, on the top floor. Aldar Properties, the company which is building the new track, has taken it for the season as a place to entertain its guests.

Overseeing the building of the new circuit, a massive undertaking, is a new challenge for Richard, who for many years was the team manager of Toyota in sports cars and more recently Formula 1. An easygoing Dubliner, Richard is one of those guys about whom no one in the paddock has a bad word to say, which is pretty rare. So he will be quite an asset for his employers when F1 comes to town. He understands how the sport works and will make sure that the teams fit in effortlessly to the circuit. When he was offered the Abu Dhabi job late last year he couldn't turn it down.

Listening to Richard it is hard not to think of the contrast with poor old Simon Gillett at Donington, who is fighting against all the financial odds to get his circuit revamped to host a race next year. Richard currently has 14,500 people working on his project, a rise of 2,500 for the summer months when, he tells me, efficiency drops off in the sweltering temperatures of 48 degrees! (I can relate to that, I'm struggling to prevent my efficiency dropping off in the current UK heatwave and I'm not having to carry a hod around.)

"We can now see that we've got a track," he said gleefully. "Our inspection by Charlie [Whiting of the FIA] is on 1 August and it has to be ready for then."

The scale of the track is what makes it different, and the imagination which has gone into the design. For example it passes underneath a hotel, and the pit exit is a tunnel. The track has a waterfront stretch which passes a deep-water harbour, like Monaco, which has 148 berths, for yachts up to 160 metres in length. As at Monaco, the boats should provide a stunning backdrop.

"It's going to put Abu Dhabi on the international map, for motorsports and tourism. The Grand Prix is part of a very big picture, a tool to activate that and a centre of excellence for motorsports," says Cregan.

The F1 circuit and the Grand Prix are only part of the story. The Yas Island will include the first Ferrari theme park, a Warner Bros theme park, a golf course and other attractions. But widening the view out further from there, the development project includes Sa'adiyat Island, which will be a centre for culture and education and Al Reem Island, which will be the financial hub. Abu Dhabi is setting the ground for the future.

Our conversation took place on the Sunday morning, barely 48 hours after FOTA had announced its breakaway from the FIA. I asked Richard whether this made him nervous, given Ferrari's involvement in Abu Dhabi, both through the theme park and the Mubadala sponsorship of the team.

"We will wait and see, like everyone else," he replied. "The Ferrari deal is not going to influence our situation."

Since then a peace deal has been struck, of course, but then thrown into some doubt again by FIA president Max Mosley. It's gone very quiet since Sunday. The Abu Dhabi deal, though, is with F1 management, so they will be hosting the F1 world championship, come what may.

Jenson Button has visited the track and he will have been delighted to hear that the expected temperature for race day on 1 November is 41 degrees, which will suit his Brawn car and the way it uses the tyres - but he may well have it all wrapped up by then.

I'm really looking forward to going to this track. It's timely because F1 is undergoing a debate about its own values and priorities in the FIA versus FOTA struggle and one of the hot topics is the extent to which new venues should replace the classic circuits. I've always been of the belief that a mix of the classic tracks like Spa and Monza with exciting new venues that really add something is what is called for. F1 must innovate, but not at the expense of its heritage.

Looks like Abu Dhabi is going to be an asset to the championship. Can't wait to see it in action.

Chapter Seven
July 2009

After the tumultuous events of late June, the ripples continued to be felt throughout July. The two sides in the power struggle finally moved closer together, ready to sign the Concorde Agreement, which would bring peace to the sport.

But there were two big shocks in store this month, with BMW abruptly deciding to withdraw and Michael Schumacher announcing a comeback after Felipe Massa's horrific accident in Budapest.

* * *

Remembering a brave F1 fan
1 July 2009

You've probably not heard of Liam Fairhurst but he was a mad-keen F1 fan and he died this week.

But there's more to it than that. Liam was only 14 and he had been battling against cancer for four years. He thought he'd beaten it, but it turned out he hadn't.

Liam was remarkable because when he was being treated the first time he made friends with another child who subsequently died. Upset by the loss of his friend, Liam was determined to raise money for Clic Sargent, the children's cancer charity, of which Eddie Jordan and I are patrons, which helps children and their families through the struggle of dealing with this horrible disease. He raised over £320,000.

Liam had an indomitable spirit. Despite being wheelchair-bound and undergoing frequent rounds of chemotherapy, radiotherapy and operations, Liam went to a lot of fund-raising events. He also won a Pride of Britain award.

He was crazy about Formula 1 and was desperate to visit the McLaren factory, which he ended up doing more than once, because Ron Dennis got involved in a bet with him to see how many fish he could catch in the lake at the factory. That turned into another big fund-raising initiative. He was a brave little guy, who proved how much you can achieve if you are really determined.

His short life really puts the struggles of the last few weeks in F1 into perspective, doesn't it?

Fernando Alonso and Ferrari
2 July 2009

Here we go again; summer's here, the temperatures are sky high, there's a long three-week gap between races and Max Mosley and FOTA have gone quiet.

If a vacuum is created something will come along to fill it and in this case it is the Spanish sports paper *AS* claiming that Ferrari is set to announce its deal with Fernando Alonso at the Italian Grand Prix in September. According to *AS*, Monza is where important Ferrari announcements are made (true up to a point) and the traditional end of season Ferrari celebration has been booked in for November at the Valencia circuit (the permanent one, not the F1 street track) in order to celebrate the arrival of the Spanish driver many in the team feel they should have hired in 2006.

"We are not going to waste our time commenting on speculation. Everyone should remember that Massa and Raikkonen have contracts which include 2010," team spokesman Luca Colajanni is quoted as saying to *Gazzetta dello Sport*.

Alonso is a Ferrari driver, the deal is done and it is looking increasingly possible that he will drive in 2010 rather than 2011. Who knows whether they will announce it at Monza, but the story fills the news vacuum at the moment.

What I will say is that this reminds me of 1995, when there were constant rumours that Michael Schumacher was going to be announced as a Ferrari driver. The Ferrari press office issued a press release on 20 June that year which said: "Ferrari would like to express, for the umpteenth time and with maximum clarity, that all stories relating to negotiations with the driver Michael Schumacher are totally false."

A few weeks later FIAT patriarch Gianni Agnelli announced the signing of Schumacher and a new era began.

On Bernie and dictators
3 July 2009

The Times has an extraordinary interview with F1 commercial boss Bernie Ecclestone today, in which he explores the theme of dictators and praises Adolf Hitler.

Ferrari boss Luca di Montezemolo recently implied that FIA president Max Mosley was a dictator and Bernie sets out here to defend the breed as people who "get things done".

"Politicians are too worried about elections," he says. "We did a terrible thing when we supported the idea of getting rid of Saddam Hussein, he was the only one who could control that country."

Warming to his theme, Bernie went on to tackle the sensitive subject of Hitler. "In the end he got lost so he wasn't a very good dictator. Either he knew what was going on and insisted, or he just went along with it – either way he wasn't a dictator."

To the Manor born
3 July 2009

I keep hearing stories about the new teams struggling to come to terms with the fact that the F1 they will be entering next year is not the same as the F1 they thought they were signing up to.

They came in on the promise of a £40 million budget cap and special rules which would give them some aerodynamic advantages over their well-established rivals and allow their Cosworth engines to run at higher revs than the other engines.

Although the deal struck between FOTA and the FIA last week will mean that F1 budgets will be dramatically reduced, it will still not be to a level anywhere near the £40 million next year which was originally on the table. The idea now for 2011 is to get down to the budget levels of the early 1990s, which was around £40 million without the engine costs, which were at least that much again.

John Booth, team principal of Manor, one of the new entrants, is quoted today in his local paper, the *Yorkshire Post* as saying, "Hopefully, it should become clearer in the next couple of weeks. There does seem an intention from all concerned to get the costs under control. We have only been planning to join Formula One for the last five or six months. Over the years it has not been feasible, you had to be a multi-, multimillionaire to even consider it."

Meanwhile Manor is currently the subject of some controversy regarding the involvement of FIA chief steward Alan Donnelly in the team's F1 entry.

According to *The Guardian*, Manor already has Virgin as a 20 per cent shareholder, which will replace the sponsorship deal with Brawn next season and Donnelly was working on finding further equity partners and sponsorship for the team in Saudi Arabia. The paper reveals details of a leaked email to illustrate the point. The email was allegedly sent on 29 May, two weeks before the FIA announced the three successful new teams.

This is part of what looks like quite a systematic attack on Donnelly, following on from the stories about him lobbying teams in Turkey, particularly Ross Brawn's, to leave FOTA's proposed breakaway and sign up to the FIA world championship.

It would appear that the tactic is both to undermine Donnelly and his FIA role by alleging conflicts of interest and possibly to force an enquiry into the process by which the entries for 2010 were made, with a view to getting the process re-run.

It's all part of the great game; the battle between FOTA and Mosley.

Bernie explains and gives F1 pause for thought
6 July 2009

Bernie Ecclestone's interview in *The Times* last weekend has brought a furious response from politicians and virtual silence from the F1 community.

Most people in F1 don't really want to get drawn into it, as they argue he shouldn't have allowed himself to get into that position in the first place. What most people don't understand is why he did the interview at all. He didn't appear to have anything to sell, no key message such as "I know the breakaway threat looked bad, but F1 is now in the best shape it's ever been in," or something of that kind. Some opinions suggest that he may have done it to help his old friend and colleague Max Mosley. But the interview certainly aroused some uncomfortable memories of last year's *News of the World* headlines and their Nazi association, which Mosley successfully challenged in court.

Actually I think what has happened here is that a couple of attractive female journalists went to Ecclestone's house and he got talking. But the whole episode does raise a subject which is extremely timely in the current debate about F1 and what direction it should take next in terms of governance.

Ecclestone went on to speak to *Bild* newspaper, the German equivalent of the *Sun*, to say that he had been misunderstood.

"All this is a big misunderstanding. In the interview we were talking about structures and that it can sometimes be good to act and make strong decisions without reservation. I wasn't using Hitler as a positive example, but pointing out that before his dreadful crimes he worked successfully against unemployment and economic problems. It was never my intention to hurt the feelings of any community. Many people in my closest circle of friends are Jewish."

Ecclestone himself is believed by many to be Jewish and on his Saturdays off he can be seen in a very famous London cafe with his largely Jewish friends, drinking coffee and chatting.

In expressing his opinion about dictators his starting point is his own experience in motor sport. It has been proven over the years that the best way to run a racing series is by a benevolent dictatorship. This is true at all levels. Someone needs to get things done and make decisions and the rest abide by them. Series run by the teams themselves don't really work, like CART in the USA for example.

F1 is where it is today because it has been run as a dictatorship. For many years the team owners like Ron Dennis, Frank Williams and even

Luca di Montezemolo were quite happy to go along with that because their series became the biggest motor sport show on earth. But now times have changed and that is what the F1 power struggle is all about.

The key to a successful dictatorship is the benevolent bit. If a tough, strong, but fair leader is in charge then things get done and it works, as long as everyone is treated equally. The teams feel that this is no longer the case, backing up their argument with examples such as the selection of new teams (with today's allegations in the *Telegraph* that having a Cosworth engine contract was a requirement for entry) to show that this system of governance has gone down the wrong track.

What the F1 teams want, motivated by the manufacturers, is a more democratic F1. This is why Max Mosley's message to the FIA members is that their institution is under threat because the Formula One Teams Association thinks it can run the sport itself. History would suggest that it would be a mistake for them to try to do that and I think that was what Bernie was trying to say (albeit obliquely) in his *Times* interview. Unfortunately he chose some bad examples to illustrate his point.

His words have upset many people it seems, but I think what will hurt him about this episode is the impression that he is out of touch, an accusation previously levelled at him over his response to the racism incident when Spanish fans mocked Lewis Hamilton.

The interesting thing will be whether anyone in F1 seeks to capitalise on this episode or whether the teams will remain focused on Mosley and his retirement in October.

Rally star Vatanen to run for FIA presidency
10 July 2009

Former world rally champion Ari Vatanen has confirmed that he will run for the FIA presidency in October.

After a week of intense negotiations it seems that the Formula One Teams Association is making it a condition of signing the new Concorde Agreement that Mosley stands by his promise at the recent FIA World Council meeting to stand down at the end of his term in October. If the teams do sign this new agreement plus a legally binding document to work together to reduce costs to early 1990s levels, Mosley may well step down.

It is thought that Mosley favours Jean Todt as his successor and Vatanen's emergence as a candidate is fascinating, as he and Todt go back many years to when the Finn used to drive for Peugeot in rally raids, like the Paris-Dakar. Vatanen has some political experience, having served as a member of the European Parliament.

"I think the time has come for a change," said Vatanen today. "My main focus is to reconcile views within the FIA and bring transparency to its stakeholders."

Having declared himself, Vatanen must now choose a cabinet of 22 people who would serve with him if elected. (As noted before, this requirement was inserted by Mosley into the FIA constitution to give him early warning of any potential rival, as once they started sounding out possible running-mates he would get to hear about it.)

Ecclestone sure that Mosley will quit
11 July 2009

Bernie Ecclestone has come out with the strongest indication yet that his old friend and colleague Max Mosley is in the final months of his FIA presidency and will stand down.

Speaking to his favourite journalist, Ed Gorman of *The Times*, Ecclestone says that Mosley will follow through on his promise when his current term is up in October.

"I have no doubt in my mind. As long as I've known Max, he's always done what he said he would do. He's an honourable person. I've always said Max can have a cheque signed by me, without any name or amount on it, because he's a trustworthy guy. So I have no doubt that he will honour all the things he's ever said he will do."

Ecclestone also underlined the reasons for Mosley's change of heart after the peace deal was agreed in Paris on 24 June; his pride was hurt by the Ferrari president painting himself as the knight who slayed the dragon.

"He was a bit upset after agreements had been made to be quiet and not throw stones at each other, and then remarks were made which upset him."

The problem, as pretty much everyone close to the situation agrees, is that egos caused the situation to flare up again, which was always a risk. But behind the scenes the businessmen have had enough of egos and are pushing hard for resolution. The current situation is hurting everyone. Ross Brawn was saying yesterday that they have sponsor deals ready to go but cannot get them to commit at the moment because they don't know what series they will be racing in.

Apparently Sir Martin Sorrell, the advertising guru and non-executive board member of F1's commercial rights holder, has been making his presence felt in the background this past couple of weeks. He also got Ecclestone to use his PR company to try to repair the fallout from the Hitler comments, hence the rumours about Peter Mandelson being involved, as the firm also acts for him.

At a cold and windy Nürburgring the various parties are moving slowly towards a conclusion to this lengthy and painful dispute. Team bosses tell me that the substantive issues are quite close to resolution, but that some details remain to be hammered out.

The teams are working closely with CVC to finalise the Concorde Agreement. One thing I have discovered is that the FIA never did manage to get the written commitment from the manufacturers behind the teams to stay in F1 until 2012. This was something Mosley was insisting on during the Silverstone weekend, but apparently it was not on the table in Paris. This leaves open the possibility that not all the manufacturers will remain in F1, despite playing key roles in the course of the dispute.

Vettel feels the pressure in home Grand Prix
11 July 2009

Sebastian Vettel was not his usual chirpy self this evening. I caught up with him at 4.30pm local time with some other media colleagues and fired a few questions at him.

I've heard from other teams' engineers that the data shows he's driving a little tentatively this weekend. No one could blame him for being cautious in the insane, changeable conditions we had this afternoon, but generally it seems that the occasion may have got to him a little bit.

This is totally understandable. He has inherited the mantle as Germany's sporting hero from Michael Schumacher so the attention on him is huge this weekend. For a 22-year-old he has handled it brilliantly; he's so calm and savvy with the media, for example, and the demands on him are many and various.

His first run in qualifying was very brave; he went out on the hard tyres and did six laps on them, with the threat of rain at any moment, whereas team-mate Mark Webber tried that and couldn't get the lap time so was forced to use up an extra set of soft tyres to get into Qualifying 2. After that, Webber had the upper hand and he got a stunning pole, 0.26 seconds faster than Vettel on an identical fuel load.

Vettel has a fast enough car to get ahead of the Brawns tomorrow, provided that he doesn't get jumped at the start by the McLarens with their KERS systems.

I asked him when he plays the tape of that lap in his mind, what is missing? "A bit of perfection here and there. It wasn't the cleanest lap. I had a couple of mistakes. And then maybe I didn't put enough effort in the lap because I was thinking I had another one so I didn't want to destroy the tyres too much so it still benefited me in the last lap. It turned out when I came around the last corner that the lights were red and I saw the chequered flag so it was pretty much over by then."

Webber powerplay heaps pressure on Brawn
12 July 2009

Mark Webber took the first win of his long career today in commanding style at the German Grand Prix, surviving a drive-through penalty for ramming Rubens Barrichello at the start and taking the chequered flag to give Red Bull its third win of the season. Webber's Red Bull team-mate, Sebastian Vettel, was second and Ferrari's Felipe Massa third.

We thought that Silverstone might have been a turning point in the season, with the almost brand new Red Bull car dominating the weekend. Today we got confirmation that it was - and it is not just because of the high speed corners that the car was quick at Silverstone. Red Bull now have the fastest car out there on any kind of circuit and as Ross Brawn and his team huddle in their debrief tonight they have a lot to chew over. Rubens Barrichello's critical outburst on the BBC is the talk of the paddock tonight and Ross Brawn looked furious when I saw him after he learned about it. This is the second time that Barrichello has come out with some strong words criticising his own team, the other occasion being Barcelona.

I can understand him being unhappy that the team switched the order of the final pit stops, giving Jenson the chance to pass him, but Jenson was faster at that stage of the race. Nevertheless it again gives a clear signal that the team wants Jenson to fight for the title and the extra point he gained here may be vital at the end of the season, given how quickly his lead is being eroded by Vettel and Webber.

But what cost Rubens a shot at victory and certainly a podium was the refuelling rig problem at his second stop. The first rig did not work so they had to go for a second one and lost time. Rubens thought he was fuelled to the finish but then found out he wasn't. I can't see Ross forgiving him for the way he spoke about the team and about Ross. He's been on the wrong end of things in the past at Ferrari and this is uncomfortable territory for both men. It's always a bad sign when team members start arguing amongst themselves in defeat and they have to rally from this low point.

Here the Brawns were beaten on pace and they were also put into a corner on race tactics, having been obliged to run a three stop strategy because they could not get the hard tyre to work and yet they could only run short stints on the soft because of the severe graining problems they encountered.

Red Bull had no such problems and were able to stick the hard tyres on Webber's car at the first stop and watch as he pulled out fantastic lap times to stay in touch with Barrichello, despite having lost 15 seconds due to the drive-through penalty.

Barrichello ran the early part of his second stint behind Massa's Ferrari and lost time, while Webber was able to reel him in.

The wider problem for Brawn is that Red Bull sensed back in March that they could win this championship and have thrown their not insignificant resources at developing their car. You never know when you are going to get another chance to win a world championship so you have to maximise your opportunities.

They have very impressive production facilities now and can turn new pieces around very quickly. The design for the Silverstone update only left Adrian Newey's desk to go into production around the time of the Monaco GP weekend.

The Brawn team has been reduced from 700 people to 450 this year, whereas Red Bull has gone the opposite way; although with budget cuts imminent for F1 the new people are all on contract, not staff, and many of them came from Brawn.

Red Bull can see that Brawn need to have one eye on saving some money for next year and they sense a weakness. The rest of the season Red Bull Racing will develop relentlessly to keep locking out these 1-2 finishes and try to take both championships. Certainly the lads on the shop floor at Red Bull think they will do it.

Of course at some point they will have to decide which of their drivers is going for the championship. At the moment with both Webber and Vettel on winning form and a gap between them of only 15 points that is a decision they cannot make. Webber reminds them that Vettel has crashed three times this year and could do so again, but Vettel has, until this weekend, been the faster driver. It's a wonderful battle and it has brought this world championship to life.

GERMAN GRAND PRIX
Nürburgring 60 laps

1. Webber	Red Bull-Renault		1h36:43.310
2. Vettel	Red Bull-Renault	+	9.252
3. Massa	Ferrari	+	15.906
4. Rosberg	Williams-Toyota	+	21.099
5. Button	Brawn-Mercedes	+	23.609
6. Barrichello	Brawn-Mercedes	+	24.468
7. Alonso	Renault	+	24.888
8. Kovalainen	McLaren-Mercedes	+	58.692

DRIVERS' STANDINGS
1. Button   68
2. Vettel   47
3. Webber   45.5
4. Barrichello   44
5. Massa   22
6. Trulli   21.5

CONSTRUCTORS' STANDINGS
1. Brawn-Mercedes   112
2. Red Bull-Renault   92.5
3. Toyota   34.5
4. Ferrari   32
5. Williams-Toyota   20.5
6. McLaren-Mercedes   14

The state of play for Webber, Button, Barrichello and Vettel
16 July 2009

On my way back from the airport on Sunday night my taxi driver was talking about Mosley this and Ecclestone that and I asked him if he was interested in other sports. He was. So then I asked him if he could name the regulatory and commercial bosses of any of those sports. He could not.

These larger-than-life characters have actually taken over the limelight from the drivers this season, which is extraordinary. However it looks as if that is about to end and the focus for the final eight races will be on who is going to win the world championship.

There are four contenders, if you include Rubens Barrichello, but he seems to think that the Brawn team doesn't want him to win the championship. In all probability, either he or Jenson Button, Mark Webber or Sebastian Vettel will be world champion. Any one of them would make a great ambassador for the sport; they are all engaging, articulate, positive people. Three of them are in the autumn of their careers (well maybe late summer) and are finding success late on, like Nigel Mansell and Mika Hakkinen did. The other is following in Lewis Hamilton's footsteps and getting it done right from the start of his career.

Mark Webber's win on Sunday was quite Mansell-esque. He was charging hard, particularly after his drive-through penalty, which handed the initiative to Barrichello. Having reviewed the live twitter feed I do during the race, there were several points when the pendulum swung the Brazilian's way, like the start and after the penalty, and then swung Mark's way, such as when Rubens was being held up by Massa in the second stint and when the fuel rig failed. It was a terrific race and despite appearances, it was not an easy win for Webber.

David Coulthard described Webber's win as the best dry weather performance of the season. It was in his Red Bull branded driver column in the *Telegraph*, so a notch down from fully impartial, but nevertheless a valid observation.

Webber is on cloud nine now and I wonder whether he will get a big kick of confidence from the win, as Mansell did in 1985 when he finally got his first win after seven years of trying.

"I've crossed the uncharted waters of pole position and victory, so that can only help, it can't be a hindrance, " said Webber. "To lead and not be the chaser was a first for me. I hope that the momentum can continue. Getting this win means that when it's close the races might seem more straightforward for me."

This last line I find very interesting. It sounds as if Webber feels he has unlocked some secret by crossing the line first on Sunday, as if the clouds of doubt and uncertainty have cleared.

In contrast I was slightly surprised to hear Button say the things he was saying after the race because they give too much away. Asked if he was worried he said:

"Wouldn't you be? I've had a sixth and a fifth the last two races. I expected more here but it was just the race didn't go our way. I expected to be on the podium, I didn't expect to beat the Red Bulls, so yeah you have to worry, but I don't think it's 'Oh sh*t we're going to lose the championship'. It's 'Come on let's make the difference'. We've got some new parts for Hungary and I'm looking forward to that. I think our car will be strong there. We don't know how strong. We'll have to wait and see.

"These are the two circuits that have been frustrating for us because of the temperatures. If we're not quick on a hot track then we've got to really worry."

You've got to admire his honesty, but Red Bull will sense a weakness. Brawn has an upgrade due for Budapest and should go well there and in Valencia, but I see no reason why they should move ahead of Red Bull unless it is a massive upgrade, like the one Red Bull brought in at Silverstone. Red Bull have a very aggressive development plan themselves. It will certainly be a fight.

Button has had luck on his side so far, with no retirements. He will do well to keep that going to the end of the season. He does of course have a 21-point cushion, too.

Another complicating factor is the increase in performance of the Ferrari and the McLaren. McLaren can qualify behind the Brawn and Red Bulls and then mess up their race by getting ahead at the start using KERS, while the Ferrari is a poor qualifying car but it can gain places with KERS, as Massa showed on Sunday. He cost Vettel any chance of a win. Button's race was wrecked by falling behind Kovalainen in the opening stint.

Vettel has been quite quiet since Sunday. He made his usual thoughtful analysis after the race and admitted that Webber had been unbeatable all weekend. But it will have been quite a sobering afternoon for him. The young German had the upper hand in that team earlier in the season, but now Webber has come back at him strongly.

The team is giving them both an equal chance, which some people have criticised. They feel that Vettel is the faster of the two and that letting Webber win on Sunday will give him a surge of confidence which might knock Vettel back. But that is racing. Vettel has already shown he's got a tough mentality and if he loses out to Webber now then he will only come back stronger next year. He has made three mistakes in races on days when Button won; he's a young charger who's right on the edge, so that's why Red Bull have hedged their bets and continue to do so.

Button, Webber, Vettel – which one will it be?

Why is Toro Rosso an ejector seat?
18 July 2009

A few readers have commented this week about the fact that Toro Rosso has one of the worst records in the field for dropping drivers. So far in their short history they have dropped Scott Speed, Tonio Liuzzi and now Sebastien Bourdais.

I've never quite got my head around Toro Rosso. It was once Minardi and was bought up by Red Bull boss Dietrich Mateschitz to fulfil several functions: to help out F1 by keeping another team on the grid, an extra non-manufacturer voice politically, an extra branding opportunity, but mainly as a place to give young drivers from the Red Bull driver development programme somewhere to learn their craft. Speed, Buemi, Vettel all fitted into this category. I suppose by definition in that situation not every move is going to work out and you will end up dropping drivers if they don't perform. But Toro Rosso do seem to have made a habit of it.

In practice they have tended to run one rookie and one driver with experience. Ironically, in 2008 they had Vettel and Bourdais, neither of whom had much F1 experience and yet the team had their best season ever! This clearly didn't go down too well at Red Bull HQ.

The problem with this situation for Toro Rosso this year, with no testing allowed, is that with a rookie in one car, Buemi, they needed someone with experience in the other seat to evaluate updates and give a strong technical direction. Bourdais, in his second year in F1 but with lots of experience from ChampCars, should have been able to do this, but clearly fell way short of expectations.

Toro Rosso is the only team yet to use a double diffuser, as the season reaches the halfway stage. This has hurt its competitiveness massively. It started the year getting cars into the third part of qualifying and now is propping up the grid. The cars will get a major upgrade in Budapest next weekend and should go substantially faster, but they will have two very inexperienced drivers bedding in the upgrade with no chance to test it first. Team boss Franz Tost says that this should bring the team back to the performance levels of the second half of the 2008 season, when Vettel won in Italy.

I think that whatever the reasons for setting up Toro Rosso in the first place, the team has become a distraction for Red Bull. They are now at F1's top table and have a real chance of winning the world title, but every penny spent on Toro Rosso is money not going into the development of this year's car and into keeping the team at the front next year.

Red Bull cut their budgets last winter, when things like the Red Bulletin F1 magazine, with an annual budget reputed to be in the €7 million range, was dropped. Both teams had cutbacks, but you sense that Toro Rosso really has been cut to the bone.

Now Red Bull are in with a shout of the title, you can tell that more resources are being thrown at the team, but this is not new funding, according to team boss Christian Horner. Funds have been reallocated from elsewhere. I wonder whether that elsewhere is Toro Rosso?

Jaime Alguersuari, the 19-year-old rookie who replaces Bourdais next week, is reputed to have a budget from Repsol of around €1 million per race for the first two races, money which will come in handy in Faenza if the Big Brother team is sucking up all the cash.

Surtees Junior perishes chasing the dream
20 July 2009

It is ironic that as a 19-year-old is given his big break into Formula 1, news comes through of an 18-year-old who died in pursuit of that same dream, while racing in Formula 2. The death of Henry Surtees, the son of 1964 world champion John, has rocked the motor sport community.

Surtees died on Sunday following a freak accident at Brands Hatch when he was hit on the head by a loose wheel, which had been knocked off the car of Jack Clarke, stepson of F1 racer Julian Bailey. Clarke had spun and hit the barriers, causing the wheel to detach.

Loose wheels have been a hot safety topic in F1 for many years, with wheel tethers being used with varying degrees of success. F1 specification wheel tethers are used on the F2 cars, but the impact was high speed and at an angle.

F2 is essentially a new category with new cars this year. It has been revived by Jonathan Palmer and the FIA, who got together with Williams F1, the designer and builder of the car.

The series features some exciting up and coming talents and is notable for a club of "sons of" F1 drivers of the past, who have all been taking steps along the road to emulate their famous fathers. Along with Surtees and Bailey, there is Alex Brundle, son of my colleague Martin and Jolyon Palmer, son of series founder Jonathan.

One can only imagine what must be going through their and their families' minds. In their day motor sport was far more dangerous than today and many of them lost close friends during their careers. Although the cars are faster now, the safety features built into them are massively superior. Many of these racing dads supervised their sons through karting and then felt comfortable with the idea of encouraging them to progress through single seaters to pursue the dream of becoming F1 drivers. This incident is a tragic reminder that you can never make racing completely safe and never believe that you are close to doing so.

Cosworth has proof its engine is competitive
23 July 2009

In the midst of all the polemics over the 2010 rules and new teams, little has been heard from Cosworth, who will be supplying the engines for all three new teams.

There are a lot of questions around Cosworth which need answering. Are they up to speed? Will the engines be reliable and competitive, seeing as they have not been in F1 since 2006? Have they got enough people? As we have seen, there have also been suggestions that having a Cosworth contract was an unspoken condition of getting an entry, so how does Cosworth feel about the way the entry process was handled?

I spoke this morning to Tim Routsis, chief executive of Cosworth and put these and other questions to him.

Cosworth has diversified since leaving F1 in 2006 to the point that none of its turnover is derived from motor sport. They have moved into aerospace and after-market automotive work. Given Cosworth's proud history in F1 it makes no sense for them to come back now and be uncompetitive. Frank Williams implied recently that he thought they would be. He felt that the manufacturer engines today were a big step ahead of the Cosworth he used in 2006 and on which the 2010 engine will be based.

Routsis reveals that his team has already carried out a test, which proves that the Cosworth engine will be competitive next season.

"There is no doubt that the teams have made some epic strides over the last few years in terms of engine reliability," he said. "The two things that really matter are that we provide a reliable and a competitive engine.

"We realised that there was no future for anybody if we rocked up with an uncompetitive engine. We wanted to verify that what we had made sense. So what we did was produce a complex model of the engine's performance as it will be in 2010 and gave it to a third party agency with the largest body of data. We asked the question, 'If you were to take all the results this year of the top three teams and substitute this engine into their cars, would it have affected the outcome of any of the races?' Because that's the ultimate measure of the competitiveness of the engine.

"The result that came back was that if the engine we are proposing for next year had been in any of the winning cars, the winning car would have still won. If it had been in any of the second place cars they would still have been second, or in one or two cases, would have won."

From what I've heard about engines this year, one of those instances may have been Toyota's second place in Bahrain. The Toyota engine is not believed to be on the same level as the Mercedes.

What helps Cosworth quite a bit is that because it has been outside F1, it is free to optimise its engine for the current regulations of 18,000rpm maximum. It was originally built for the 20,000rpm rules of 2006, but has undergone substantial internal changes. The existing engines have all been retuned from the old 19,000rpm rules, with tight restrictions on areas that could be worked on, restrictions which don't apply to Cosworth.

"It will be a lot more fuel efficient, it will obviously be retuned to the 18,000rpm limit as opposed to the 20,000rpm limit and we are doing quite a lot of work to make sure that it is optimised to give a competitive engine," continues Routsis. "So whilst you would be able to put the two engines side by side and see a family resemblance, there is a lot of difference in the detail.

"We are picking all of the things from the last three years that make sense and putting them in the engine. We have been given the opportunity to do a proper retune. A lot of activity that our competitors have been carrying out in the last three years has been an enormous amount of focus on areas which they were allowed to deal with, which represent small gains for enormous effort. We are trying to make sure that the things we focus on are the ones which give the big gains."

Cosworth shed 200 people after its 2006 withdrawal but Routsis claims that "the core kernel of the brains trust" was kept, in other words the core engineering team is the same as before. However, he adds, "There is no doubt that we need more people to service three teams and to that end we are recruiting at the moment in the areas of track support and engine build."

As regards the cost to the customer, Cosworth is supplying 20 engines per team next year for £5 million, according to the rules of 8 race engines per driver per season plus test engines. But the business model requires them to supply three teams and Routsis is expecting all three to honour their contracts. "We have very clear contracts with them and they expect us to honour our commitments and we expect that to be a reciprocal arrangement."

There have been persistent rumours that USF1 is thinking about using Toyota engines.

As for the controversy over the entry process, Routsis believes that the due diligence process the FIA carried out on the new teams was thorough and that high profile teams which failed to make the cut did so because they either didn't have an engine contract in place, as the rules required, or were unable to prove adequate funding for a minimum of three years, despite what they may have implied about needing a Cosworth deal to win an entry.

The new teams selection process, and by extension the involvement of Cosworth, became embroiled in the ferocious political fight between FOTA and the FIA and as with any war the first casualty was truth. No doubt in the coming months we will discover exactly how the new teams were selected.

"There's far too much emotion in the debate and in a lot of instances the issues have been lost sight of and it has become a personality debate," says Routsis.

Massa says Alguersuari debut is wrong
23 July 2009

Felipe Massa is one of a number of drivers to react with concern to the debut of 19-year-old Jaime Alguersuari in the Toro Rosso. Alguersuari has done very little mileage in an F1 car, and what he has done was in a straight line, but he qualifies for a superlicence because he won last season's British F3 championship.

"For me he's too young," said Massa. "He's never driven a Formula 1 car, or he has driven it in a straight line, or whatever. For me it's wrong. It's not good for him. He can burn himself very quickly."

Massa started at the age of 20 with Sauber, but had enjoyed a whole winter of testing before his first race. He had a troubled first year and was dropped by Sauber, so went to Ferrari as a test driver. He has never really shaken off the tag of wild child he picked up in that incident-filled first season, despite fighting for last year's championship.

It is a huge ask for Alguersuari. To learn even simple things like the steering wheel will take time, as Jenson Button pointed out.

"It's not just about driving quick, there's a lot more to it and I'm sure that he doesn't understand all the electronics on an F1 car. The steering wheel to start with is very complicated and to get the pit stops sorted in two days is going to be very difficult. There's a lot to learn and a lot to take in. Not having driven an F1 car around a circuit, I'm surprised he's been allowed to race this weekend. I say good luck to him - it's a risk he's willing to take and for his sake I hope he does a good job."

I have heard both Button and Massa say in the past that on reflection they came in too young, but both survived and have had long careers.

We will all be watching to see how early, or late, Alguersuari brakes for turn one on his first flying lap tomorrow. It will tell us a lot. I expect him to do a lot of laps on Friday.

Alguersuari's fellow Spaniard, Fernando Alonso, was more positive than Massa or Button, saying that the young man is a talent and should not worry about his age or inexperience. "I'm in favour of beginning as young as possible", said the man who once held the record as the youngest pole-sitter, winner and world champion, before even younger men came along. Such is the march of the youth cult in F1.

Felipe Massa suffers horrific accident
25 July 2009

Felipe Massa has been operated on this evening and is now in an induced coma in the AEK Hospital in Budapest. The 28-year-old Brazilian was hit on the head by a metal spring weighing 700 grammes, which had fallen from the rear suspension of Rubens Barrichello's Brawn car. The incident happened during qualifying. Massa was heading back to the pits and was four seconds behind Barrichello on the road, when the spring became detached. It bounced down the road and hit Massa on the left side of his forehead. He was briefly knocked unconscious and his feet went on to the brake and throttle simultaneously before he ploughed into the barriers.

An inaccurate report from AP this evening suggested that his condition was life-threatening but this is not the case. The operation was successful and he is likely to be woken tomorrow.

Medical estimates of how long he will be out of action vary from two months upwards. It has been suggested by one doctor here that he may miss the rest of the season. More will be known when the medically induced coma ends and the medics can assess the amount of bruising to the front of the brain.

The data says that he applied 60bar of pressure to the brake, which is the equivalent of laying his foot on it gently, while the throttle was effectively jammed on.

Ross Brawn tonight explained that the spring was from the third damper and is made of steel. "The damper is still attached but the cap had come off and the spring escaped," said Brawn. "I don't know the full details but it was a freak accident."

Brawn replaced the spring on Jenson Button's car just in case, but said that this did not affect the balance of the car for Button's final qualifying run. He said that he had never experienced a spring detaching itself in all his years in F1 engineering. He added that he thought that the work done on making helmets safer had been essential in this situation.

Hamilton takes surprise win in Hungary
26 July 2009

Lewis Hamilton won the Hungarian Grand Prix today, heading home Ferrari's Kimi Raikkonen and Red Bull's Mark Webber.

Although many predicted a strong start for Hamilton after qualifying fourth, few would have guessed that he would drive away from the field in the race, his car handling both the soft and supersoft tyres very consistently.

He made a move on Webber into turn one for second place at the start, but ran wide and Webber re-passed him. Hamilton came back at him however and grabbed second place again. At the front, pole-sitter Fernando Alonso led in the Renault, but his challenge ended on lap 13 when his front wheel came off following a pit stop.

Raikkonen had an eventful start, which the stewards are looking at now, making some sharp moves into turn one and colliding with Sebastian Vettel in turn two. The damage to Vettel's suspension ultimately caused it to fail and Vettel retired before half distance. Raikkonen claimed to have no idea that he and Vettel had made contact and the team did not tell him about the investigation.

Webber struggled for pace on the soft tyre in the middle section of the race and seemed to settle for third place, knowing that he would move into second place in the championship ahead of Vettel. He said that he would not be asking the team to back his championship challenge following this result. "It's too soon for that," he said, rather unconvincingly.

Points leader Jenson Button finished a disconsolate 7th after another difficult day when the Brawn could not get the tyres working properly. Button has had three bad results in a row and this one is particularly hard to swallow because it was on a track where the team should have shone, with a major upgrade to the car and with the hot temperatures which suited their car at the start of the season. Yet the car had no pace today.

Hamilton's win was a reward for an amazing amount of work by the McLaren team. They have been bringing parts out all weekend, some designed as recently as last week and they have a win to show for their efforts. They should go quite well in Valencia, but on the high speed aero tracks like Spa, they will still struggle to match the Red Bull car.

Ferrari meanwhile have endured a tough weekend with the accident to Felipe Massa. Team principal Stefano Domenicali was at the hospital all morning, only coming to the track just before the start of the race.

Raikkonen couldn't get close enough to Hamilton to strike, but it was noticeable that he was able to match his pace for much of the race. Hamilton's advantage was largely built in the opening laps.

Formula 1 now takes a summer break and the teams are forced to close their factories for two weeks during this time, so development will be limited before the next race in Valencia.

HUNGARIAN GRAND PRIX
Budapest 70 laps

1. Hamilton	McLaren-Mercedes		1h38:23.876
2. Raikkonen	Ferrari	+	11.529
3. Webber	Red Bull-Renault	+	16.886
4. Rosberg	Williams-Toyota	+	26.967
5. Kovalainen	McLaren-Mercedes	+	34.392
6. Glock	Toyota	+	35.237
7. Button	Brawn-Mercedes	+	55.088
8. Trulli	Toyota	+	1:08.172

DRIVERS' STANDINGS

1. Button   70
2. Webber   51.5
3. Vettel   47
4. Barrichello 44
5. Rosberg   25.5
6. Trulli   22.5

CONSTRUCTORS' STANDINGS

1. Brawn-Mercedes   114
2. Red Bull-Renault   98.5
3. Ferrari   40
4. Toyota   38.5
5. McLaren-Mercedes   28
6. Williams-Toyota   25.5

Renault banned from European Grand Prix
26 July 2009

Renault have been banned from next month's European Grand Prix after Fernando Alonso's right-front wheel came off during today's Hungarian Grand Prix. The ban means the Spaniard will now miss his home race on the streets of Valencia.

Alonso had been leading the race from pole position when he emerged from his first pit stop without his right-front wheel sufficiently fitted. Alonso tried to recover and get to the pits, however the wheel freed itself and bounced off into the barriers.

The penalty is very severe and probably would not have been given had the Henry Surtees and Felipe Massa incidents not happened recently. But in this climate of heightened sensitivity to flying objects, the stewards felt that by allowing the car to continue until the wheel came loose, Renault had not taken sufficient regard for safety.

However, to penalise Mark Webber with a drive-through last week and not hit Kimi Raikkonen with a similar penalty for his actions at the start today when he made contact with Sebastian Vettel seems inconsistent.

Renault have appealed against the decision with a hearing likely to take place during the summer break.

BMW pulls out, but team should survive
29 July 2009

BMW today became the second major manufacturer to quit Formula 1 in eight months. I never much liked the way they went about their racing, being too focused on corporate targets and not enough on racing. But I see no reason why the team, based in Hinwil, should not be on the grid next year in a new guise.

The timing of the BMW board's decision was motivated by the imminent need for a signature on the new Concorde Agreement. It has been agreed between all parties and was simply awaiting main board approval from two manufacturers, one of whom was BMW.

That approval was not forthcoming and so they have been forced to withdraw now rather than commit themselves to the sport until the end of 2012. It remains to be seen if any other manufacturer will feel unable to make such a commitment. Toyota moved this evening to make it clear that they will not follow in BMW's wake. "Through cost reduction we will continue our Formula 1 activities. Our situation remains unchanged, " said a statement.

In some ways BMW's withdrawal is a shock, in other ways not. Along with Toyota and Renault, BMW were frequently cited as manufacturers whose long-term commitment to the sport was questionable. FIA president Max Mosley has been warning for some time that the sport could not be allowed to depend on the whim of manufacturers who come and go as it suits them, and that new teams were needed to ensure its stability.

The obvious answer as to how to achieve this was to cut the costs of competing dramatically. His chosen route of an enforced budget cap almost brought about the destruction of the sport with a walkout from eight teams, but in the end a compromise has been reached with a legally binding agreement between teams to keep costs at around £80 million next year and £40 million the year after.

With commercial revenues from the sport and from sponsors far exceeding this figure, teams are set to become profit centres rather than cost centres and so one has to regard the withdrawal today as not being primarily about economics. It's about damage to the BMW brand from performing so poorly this year and possibly some disillusionment about the way the sport has been managed.

Results have played a significant part in their decision; the team was on an impressive upward curve in 2006-2008, but I always thought that they bottled it last year, choosing to work on the 2009 car once they had achieved their 2008 targets of a first win and third in the constructors' championship, rather than throw the kitchen-sink at trying to win the title with Kubica. They had the chance: Ferrari and McLaren were making lots of mistakes. That was not the decision of a racer, rather of a corporate entity too focused on targets and now with the results frankly embarrassing, they have pulled the plug.

"It only took us three years to establish ourselves as a top team," said Klaus Draeger, one of the BMW board members. "Unfortunately, we were unable to meet expectations in the current season."

This outcome is a huge personal failure for Mario Theissen, the team principal, who steered BMW away from an engine supply deal with Williams and into running its own team. It shows the pressure he must have been under from the board to get results and why he played it so cautiously over the last few years.

"Of course, we, the employees in Hinwil and Münich, would all have liked to continue this ambitious campaign and show that this season was just a hiccup following three successful years," he said. "But I can understand why this decision was made from a corporate perspective. We will now focus sharply on the remaining races and demonstrate our fighting spirit and put in a good result as we bid farewell to Formula 1 racing."

Peter Sauber is the man who must be hurting the most. I interviewed him in the early 2000s and he said that his main objective was to secure the future for his employees. He chose BMW because he believed in their stability and long-term commitment. I always wondered why the team remained "BMW Sauber" and he retained his shareholding, and now I wonder whether he might do a Ross Brawn and take over the team for 2010. The sport would retain an important team and Sauber would be able to operate on £40 million a year going forward. The circumstances for such a move are far less risky now than they were for Brawn during the winter of 2009, with far more certainty of what F1 will cost.

BMW is likely to be able to sell the team to a new investor once the Concorde Agreement is signed; for Sauber may not want to take the investment on himself, as he is not a young man. But in my view, BMW owes it to the sport to set Sauber up in the same way as Honda set up Brawn and let the racing continue.

Schumacher confirms shock comeback
29 July 2009

Seven-times world champion Michael Schumacher has confirmed that he will make a sensational return to Formula 1 as a replacement for Felipe Massa, in an amazing turn of events.

The German has previously rejected any suggestion of a return to the sport; however, a sense of loyalty to the team in its time of need has inspired his return.

"The most important thing first: thank God, all news concerning Felipe is positive. I wish him all the best," said Schumacher.

"I was meeting this afternoon with Stefano Domenicali and Luca di Montezemolo and together we decided that I will prepare myself to take the place of Felipe.

"Though it is true that the chapter of Formula One has been closed for me for a long time, it is also true that for loyalty reasons to the team I cannot ignore that unfortunate situation. But as the competitor I am I also very much look forward to facing this challenge."

A Ferrari statement said Schumacher would undertake a specific training programme to ensure that he is up to full fitness. Should he pass, he'll take over from the European Grand Prix on 23 August.

Schumacher's last race in Brazil in 2006 was a masterpiece, even though the result doesn't look that way. He was miles faster than anyone else that day and it was the perfect way to sign off. Three years have passed and he's clearly not been fulfilled by life after F1.

Ferrari have a moment of great need and he clearly feels close to them. It is not ideal for him to return at such short notice and he will be driving on a track he doesn't know. But the car was good enough for a podium in Budapest last weekend and the sport will be electrified by his return.

At a time when drivers are getting younger, we would have a 40-year-old competing in a Grand Prix, with a driver born in the 1960s sharing the grid with one born in the 1990s. Formula 1's capacity to surprise never ends. I'll have to write a new chapter to the biography and I wouldn't bet against Schumacher winning.

Chapter Eight
August 2009

August was the month of Michael Schumacher's abortive comeback. I was in Italy when the story broke and he did his controversial test in a 2007 car. There was a palpable sense of excitement, which quickly turned to disappointment when he pulled out with neck problems. This is turn gave rise to Ferrari's strange decision to give Luca Badoer the drive, the veteran proving something of an "Eddie the Eagle", battling hard for last place.

It was also the month when the Concorde Agreement was finally signed after years of wrangling.

But the month kicked off with an extraordinary outburst from a driver against his former boss, which would have huge repercussions on the sport the following month. Nelson Piquet Jr called Flavio Briatore his "executioner". Ironically that is exactly what Piquet turned out to be for Briatore.

* * *

Piquet lets Briatore have it with both barrels
3 August 2009

Nelson Piquet's demise as a Renault driver has been coming for some time. Today he got the bullet and reacted by issuing a strongly worded statement about how unfair his treatment had been at the hands of Flavio Briatore, the team's principal as well as Piquet's manager. On the face of it the young Brazilian's F1 career appears to be over, in the sense that it is hard to see another team taking him on.

Piquet's success in motor sport has largely come in the family environment of his own team, both in F3 and GP2. He has not impressed during his season and a half in F1. He claims this is because he was not given the same conditions as team-mate Fernando Alonso. Looking at it from the outside, with information sources from within the team, I myself think the team gave him plenty of opportunities to prove himself. Many teams would have dropped him after his poor showing in the 2008 season. He had some good days, even beating Alonso on the odd occasion, but the engineers know the truth and both the Renault guys and the engineers from other teams reckoned that he just isn't good enough.

Of course that is not how Piquet sees it. "The conditions I have had to deal with during the last two years have been very strange to say the least – there are incidents that I can hardly believe occurred myself. If I now need to give explanations, I am certain it is because of the unfair situation I have been in the past two years.

"I always believed that having a manager was being a part of a team and having a partner. A manager is supposed to encourage you, support you, and provide you with opportunities. In my case it was the opposite. Flavio Briatore was my executioner.

"On numerous occasions, fifteen minutes before qualifying and races, my manager and team boss [Briatore] would threaten me, telling me if I didn't get a good result, he had another driver ready to put in my place."

Piquet joins a list of disgruntled drivers who have found that being the number two driver in a Briatore team is not easy. That list includes Johnny Herbert, JJ Lehto, Alex Wurz and Jarno Trulli, all of whom had unhappy experiences. Piquet says that he was not given equal treatment or equipment to Alonso in 2008 and that this continued in 2009 despite promises of future equality. "For the 2009 season Briatore ... promised me everything would be different, that I would get the attention I deserved but had never received, and that I would get 'at least equal treatment' inside the team," he added.

I can see why a team would give a development part to Alonso if only one was available, but they would want to score maximum points in the constructors' championship and you don't do that by holding one driver back. Alonso is so vastly superior to Piquet as a driver that he wouldn't have needed any technical advantages.

However I can see how the lack of an arm around the shoulder in Piquet's case was a problem. My own view on Piquet is that he can be very fast but that he needs too much preparation time and testing to hit the performance peaks, particularly in qualifying, whereas a top F1 driver can just get in and nail it straightaway. Compare Piquet with a driver of similar F1 experience, like Sebastian Vettel, and you will see what I mean.

Romain Grosjean is expected to replace Piquet at Valencia, if the team is allowed to race there, or at Spa if they are not. For 2010 the feeling is that Renault's number one target is Robert Kubica.

Thoughts on the new Concorde Agreement
4 August 2009

War is over, at least for a short while.

On Friday night the teams, the FIA and the F1 commercial rights holder signed the new Concorde Agreement, which runs until the end of 2012. With the signing of this agreement, stability is returned to F1. There will be no breakaway series, no more new rules being imposed on teams. Instead the F1 commission will be restored, which gives the teams a say in the shaping of new rules.

It has been an immensely damaging period for the image of the sport, with polemics, breakaway threats and constant instability. Just how damaging will become clear in the next few months when we see if any new sponsors and major corporations are attracted to come in and invest.

After so much strife the wording of the FIA's statement was interesting. Max Mosley was portrayed as presidential, his cause helped by the shock pull out last week of BMW, which reminded everyone of how manufacturers can behave and why Mosley went to war with them on costs in the first place.

"Following approval by the World Motor Sport Council, late last night FIA President Max Mosley signed the 2009 Concorde Agreement, heralding a renewed period of stability for the FIA Formula One world championship," said the FIA's statement.

"The new Concorde Agreement, which runs until 31 December 2012, provides for a continuation of the procedures in the 1998 Concorde Agreement, with decisions taken by working groups and commissions, upon which all teams have voting rights, before going to the WMSC for ratification."

The problem is that next time around the teams are committed to achieving a much improved share of the commercial revenues from the sport, which will set them on a collision course with Bernie Ecclestone and his partners CVC. Some say the figure they will look for is as high as 80 per cent.

So we will have stability for a couple of years and then the fighting will start again in earnest. We will also have a new FIA president in October, in all probability Jean Todt, so the dynamics will be different there and he may well want to make his mark on the next Concorde Agreement.

There are some senior team figures in F1 who believe that they should all sit down now and agree a deal to run from 2013 to 2023, capitalising on the rare spirit of togetherness, which led to the new deal. But it's hard to imagine the manufacturers wanting to commit themselves for that long this far out.

I think everyone at the top in F1 shocked themselves with the breakaway decision during Silverstone weekend and will be very keen to avoid a repeat. But at the same time the teams feel that it is wrong for so much of the commercial revenues of the sport to go into servicing CVC's $2.6 billion debt (some $300 million per year) rather than being shared out among the participants.

So let's enjoy the few moments' peace before the next showdown.

How McLaren turned a dog into a winner
8 August 2009

"No one needed this win more than me," said McLaren Mercedes team principal Martin Whitmarsh in the immediate aftermath of Lewis Hamilton's win in Budapest on 26 July.

We were standing in the McLaren motorhome, with Michael Jackson's "Bad" pumping out of the stereo. A pressure release valve had popped off and the team was in the mood for celebration.

The team has changed a lot since Whitmarsh took over in March. There is always a cool playlist on the go whenever you go into their hospitality area, concocted by music loving press officer Steve Cooper. The air of tension which always hung over the team when Dennis was around has palpably lifted, despite the amount of pressure on Whit-marsh personally this year.

Almost immediately after he took over the team got itself into a mess over misleading the Melbourne stewards.

Since then Whitmarsh has found himself being pulled in different directions with the need to commit significant time to the FOTA cause, time he wasn't then spending on making McLaren stronger.

There was pressure too from the sponsors, who were not happy with the team's lack of competitiveness. They still have to get their place back at the front of the grid next season, but this win was a welcome boost in a season which had looked pretty dire.

Schumacher forced to call off dream comeback
11 August 2009

Michael Schumacher will not drive the Ferrari at the European Grand Prix on 23 August, nor at any of the remaining races of 2009. The much discussed comeback is officially off. Ferrari president Luca di Montezemolo confirmed this morning that test driver Luca Badoer will take the seat at Valencia, and then we will see what happens for the remaining races.

Schumacher always said that his comeback was subject to passing medical tests on his neck, which he injured in a motorbike accident earlier this year. Everyone had got terribly carried away with the story and conveniently forgotten that there was a chance he wouldn't be fit.

At the time the extent of his injuries was not given and when I asked his assistant Sabine Kehm last week about this she said that this had been deliberate, which indicated that perhaps they were more serious than merely bruising or a strain. He was moving stiffly in the neck and shoulders when he came to Grands Prix recently in his role as Ferrari consultant.

In his statement today on his website he says, "The consequences of the injuries caused by the bike-accident in February, fractures in the area of head and neck, unfortunately have turned out to be still too severe. The word "fractures" explains the reason why he isn't coming back and why Kehm was so keen to manage expectations last week when she said that the comeback was not certain, but subject to medical checks.

His test at Mugello recently was to evaluate his physical condition and to test his neck. He was due to test again this week, but clearly the medical examinations have revealed to him that it was not worth it. He said that the deal with his wife Corinna was that his health had to be the number one priority in any comeback and it is clearly the case that this could not be guaranteed should he race an F1 car in his current condition.

The statement on his website shows the depth of his regret, "I really tried everything to make that temporary comeback possible, however, much to my regret it didn't work out. Unfortunately we did not manage to get a grip on the pain in the neck which occurred after the private test in Mugello, even if medically or therapeutically we tried everything possible.

"I am disappointed to the core. I am awfully sorry for the guys of Ferrari and for all the fans which crossed their fingers for me. I can only repeat that I tried everything that was within my power. All I can do now is to keep my fingers crossed for the whole team for the coming races."

Ferrari president Luca di Montezemolo expressed his disappointment that Schumacher would not race again,

"I am very unhappy that a problem means that Michael cannot return to racing," commented Luca di Montezemolo. "In the past few days, I could appreciate his great efforts and extraordinary motivation which had spread through the team and fans around the world. No doubt his return would have been good for Formula One and I am sure it would have seen him fighting for wins again."

Badoer was passed over for the stand-in role in 1999, when Schumacher broke his leg. His presence in the car will make it more difficult for Ferrari to achieve its goal of third place in the championship.

Montezemolo's comments about Schumacher and his extraordinary motivation are aimed at Kimi Raikkonen, who now leads the Ferrari team and on whose shoulders their fortunes rest this season. The team needs him to step up and win a race for them. Raikkonen's response on track will be interesting to monitor.

Grosjean needs to put demons behind him on debut
20 August 2009

Romain Grosjean is the first Frenchman for over 20 years to drive for Renault. It's a great honour for him and one for which he has waited patiently.

He seems very excited about his opportunity, but according to people who have observed him closely, he has some demons which he needs to overcome if he is to make the most of his chance and establish himself as a Renault driver for 2010. Apparently the huge accident he suffered in GP2 at Monaco this year really shook him up and his season has clearly been affected by it. Obviously it's not the ideal preparation for the biggest moment of your career, but the whole point of being a racing driver is to challenge fate, to make things happen for yourself.

I spoke to former racer Jacques Lafitte about Grosjean today and he made the observation that the Swiss-born Frenchman is a real "warrior", in that he has that rage in his driving which champions must have. But he has appeared to be too aggressive this season in GP2. Lafitte wonders whether Grosjean might be one of those drivers who pushes too hard in the feeder series, but then delivers a more measured performance when he takes the step up to F1, rather like Jean Alesi did in 1989. We will see.

Fernando Alonso said today that he felt Nelson Piquet's problem was not a lack of talent, on that score Alonso rates him. Rather, he felt that Piquet wasn't able to establish the relationships with the people in the team to get the most out of them, himself and the equipment. Grosjean has been part of the Renault set-up for longer and he will be looking for the team to help him make the most of this chance.

Kubica learned of BMW decision by email!
20 August 2009

Robert Kubica had a wry grin on his face this afternoon when a few of us caught up with him. The Pole has had a couple of weeks to digest the news that his BMW team will not be in F1 next year and this means upheaval and change for him. He knows that it's a case of what might have been, but he also has to look forwards.

Astonishingly the way he heard about the news was first from an internet site which ran a speculative piece before the announcement and then soon after he received an email telling him the news. Not a phone call, an email. Needless to say he wasn't too impressed with this.

There is a terrible irony for Kubica about the way BMW's demise has come about. He was pushing for the team to throw everything at developing the 2008 car as he felt that they had the chance to win the title and that you never know when that chance may come again. I remember his anger as the season ebbed away from him, the corporate non-racer mentality of the management having decided to focus on 2009 and only those developments which had carry-over potential.

This year hasn't been as good as last year in terms of showcasing Kubica's abilities. He has at times been outperformed by team-mate Nick Heidfeld, which wasn't the case in 2008. Nevertheless his stock is still pretty high in F1.

Renault would dearly love to have Kubica, because he is one of the few really strong drivers potentially available. Bear in mind that they are looking for a new title sponsor to replace ING and any new sponsor is likely to want to know who the drivers will be before signing on the dotted line. Kovalainen and Grosjean, for example, might not stir their blood like Kubica would.

Kubica is not worried for himself, but rather for the mechanics and staff at the team headquarters in Hinwil. Efforts are ongoing to save the team, but it's being said in Germany that BMW were looking for €65 million for the team, which is a high price when you consider that Honda sold their team to its management for £1.

Vettel signs Red Bull contract extension
21 August 2009

Sebastian Vettel will be a Red Bull driver for at least another two seasons, with an option to stay for 2012 as well.

The 22-year-old German has developed in the last 12 months into one of the sport's leading drivers and with Red Bull producing a race-winning car this year the combination has become very strong.

His decision to stay is no great surprise but it is timely as the driver market is really starting to intensify now and this announcement needed to be made to stop any further speculation about Vettel's future. Mark Webber was recently confirmed for another year so Red Bull has a very strong driver line-up. The key for them now is to stay at F1's top table on a technical level. In Adrian Newey they have a first-class engineering boss and there is no reason why they should go backwards next year with so much stability. The same question has to be asked about Brawn; can they keep it up?

This year the definition of what constitutes a "top team" has been blurred, with Ferrari, McLaren and Renault dropping behind Red Bull and Brawn. But the rate of progress at McLaren in particular indicates that next year they will be stronger.

Interestingly if you compare the tone of the Vettel announcement with the one made about Webber recently, the headline today announces "Vettel commits to Red Bull", which very much talks up the driver, whereas the Webber one simply stated "Webber to drive for Red Bull" which is quite neutral (and unimaginative!).

There seems to be a subtle slant towards Vettel in that team because he is the product of the young driver programme rather than an experienced gun for hire as Webber is. This makes the close battle between them all the more fascinating as Webber stubbornly digs in and keeps delivering the results.

What to do about a problem like Badoer?
22 August 2009

Pity poor Luca Badoer; he pounds around test-tracks at the wheel of championship-winning Ferraris for years, dreaming of his chance to race one of the blood-red cars in a Grand Prix. When the call comes from President Montezemolo he has "no choice" in his words but to accept and travel to Valencia, to a track he does not know, to qualify and race a car for the first time in ten years when he hasn't been able to test. The dream turns into a nightmare.

In third practice, the last one before qualifying, he was just under two seconds slower than team-mate Kimi Raikkonen and a second slower than Jaime Alguersuari, the next slowest car. But instead of moving closer in qualifying he went backwards, dropping to an embarrassing 2.6 seconds behind Raikkonen and 1.5 seconds behind a 19-year-old in only his second Grand Prix.

Where do you start to try to work out how this situation arose and what Ferrari do about it? To start with, if the excuse is that he hasn't driven a car for almost a year, then why not stick him in the 2007 Ferrari that Michael Schumacher drove at Mugello and let him shake off the rust? If the excuse is that he is race rusty, scan the racing calendar, pick up the phone and stick him in a race somewhere.

Most of the ex-F1 drivers I have quizzed about this say that they would have said yes if Ferrari had called, because that is in the nature of a racing driver; you want to race and to race a Ferrari is, literally, a dream. But beyond that they are all agreed that the decision by Montezemolo – and it was him, not Stefano Domenicali, who made the call – is a mistake and that of the available active drivers Nelson Piquet would have been the best choice to back up Raikkonen. (Such a choice would also have provided some useful data on the relative performances of Raikkonen and Alonso, but that's another story.) Marc Gene, the team's other test driver, is active, he won Le Mans, but the feeling is that he is not as fast as Badoer.

Montezemolo was quoted in the Italian media on Friday as saying that Badoer could win this race. "We will win with a man from Veneto," he said.

I went to Badoer's press briefing this afternoon and he was putting a brave face on it, saying that "This track is new for me and it's very difficult. So our expectation was more or less where we are today. I need to drive, to get confidence with the car. I ask you to be patient, because I'm not a robot or Superman. I'm human and I need time to get quick."

The team has been very supportive and the feeling I get is that he will indeed treat the race as a test and then at Spa and Monza, which he knows like the back of his hand, he will be expected to be closer. The pressure at Monza, though, will be pretty intense.

The German media continues to ramp up the talk of Michael Schumacher making his comeback at a later stage in the season, possibly after Monza, but sources close to the driver say that it's unlikely. It doesn't do Schumacher any harm commercially to be the centre of attention again and, as he himself always says, "Never say never."

What does Button have to do now?
25 August 2009

Jenson Button had another low key weekend in Valencia, his fourth poor race in a row. It's not the end of the world, championships are won by keeping the scoreboard ticking over and Button has at least scored in every race.

But unlike the previous races, Valencia was a race where Brawn had the fastest car – for the first time really since Monaco – and this meant a chance to take a much needed win or podium to release some of the pressure which has been building on him.

Instead Rubens Barrichello was the faster car all weekend, qualified well on a high fuel load and won the race. Jenson made a mistake in qualifying when his finger was jolted as he went over a kerb and he went up two gears by mistake. That put him fifth on the grid. With Vettel retiring and Kovalainen fading, he should have finished third at worst. However he was tentative at the start and from there he raced to seventh place.

After the race he said that he would be more aggressive in Spa, which is a message he needed to send out, because what we saw at the start in Valencia gave the opposition a clear message that he was thinking of the championship as he steered into the first corner.

Vettel might have been expected to be doing the same, but there was a whisper around the pit lane before the race that his engine might not last so he had nothing to lose. Button knew this.

Neither do Raikkonen or Rosberg, who surged past Button, have anything to lose. They are not in the championship fight. Button is likely to find himself surrounded by the same characters in Spa, where the Red Bull should be the fastest car again and he will be scrapping for a podium.

However the picture is more complicated; with this win, Rubens Barrichello is now most certainly in the championship hunt. It was his first win for five years and he's had the upper hand on Jenson lately. This result adds to Jenson's woes because with Vettel and Mark Webber breathing down his neck, he would be thinking that soon the Brawn team's main effort would be focusing on him for the title. Instead Barrichello's win has opened up the championship again and made Jenson's life more complicated.

"It is better to be consistent and not crash, but if you are consistent and get two points it is not enough," said Button after the race. "I am going to go to Spa and be more aggressive, for sure. This was the first time when we have had a strong car that I have not been able to get the most out of it."

Button looked pretty edgy all weekend. You can tell a lot from a driver's body language and he has looked remarkably relaxed at times when you would have expected him to be jumpy. Last weekend, after a nice long break, with a big points lead and knowing he had the fastest car there, he should have looked a lot more at ease than he did.

Perhaps the realisation that the finish line is in sight and the greatest dream of his life is within reach, could have made him tense up a bit. We saw the same thing with Damon Hill in 1996. But he came through in the end.

* * *

Renault took part in the European Grand Prix after winning its appeal against the Hungarian stewards' decision.

EUROPEAN GRAND PRIX
Valencia 57 laps

1. Barrichello	Brawn-Mercedes	1h35:51.289
2. Hamilton	McLaren-Mercedes	+ 2.358
3. Raikkonen	Ferrari	+ 15.994
4. Kovalainen	McLaren-Mercedes	+ 20.032
5. Rosberg	Williams-Toyota	+ 20.870
6. Alonso	Renault	+ 27.744
7. Button	Brawn-Mercedes	+ 34.913
8. Kubica	BMW Sauber	+ 36.667

DRIVERS' STANDINGS
1. Button   72
2. Barrichello   54
3. Webber   51.5
4. Vettel   47
5. Rosberg   29.5
6. Hamilton   27

CONSTRUCTORS' STANDINGS
1. Brawn-Mercedes   126
2. Red Bull-Renault   98.5
3. Ferrari   46
4. McLaren-Mercedes   41
5. Toyota   38.5
6. Williams-Toyota   29.5

Spa – the joy of a real race track!
27 August 2009

Just arrived at Spa on an early BA flight from Heathrow. Ross Brawn and some of his senior engineers were on it too as well as some of the photographers.

Then there is a 90-minute drive from Brussels to Spa, which is about half an hour south of the city of Liège. Amazingly it's a beautiful day here. I've been coming to Spa for the Grand Prix for 20 years and I can count on my fingers the number of times I've seen a hot sunny day here. Let's hope it lasts. The forecast is for it to stay sunny or partly cloudy all weekend, with a high of around 22 degrees.

I always love that moment when you drive down the forest track which leads to the car park here and there in front of you is your first sight of Eau Rouge. It's like seeing a favourite mountain.

I used to stand up there with the legendary journo Denis Jenkinson and he could always tell the top six just from the way they went through the corner. He was always right.

This track is very special and it's special to me because it's a track where my Dad, Bill, always did really well. He was a works Lotus driver in the late 1950s and early 1960s and also ran the Lotus sports car team competing in Le Mans, Spa 24 hours and all the big events. He told me all about this place long before I ever came here and I have always loved it.

One of my strongest memories of this place is the time when Kimi Raikkonen was battling with Michael Schumacher for pole position. It was 2002 and Olivier Panis had blown an engine in the BAR at Radillon, at the top of Eau Rouge, which meant that there was a curtain of dense white smoke sitting on the hill. Raikkonen plunged into it without lifting, or seeming to care where in that pall of smoke the stationary BAR might be. It was one of the bravest and most committed pieces of driving I've ever seen. Raikkonen always goes well here and even though they have stopped developing the Ferrari I think he'll get a good result, especially as the KERS will help him on the long run from Eau Rouge to Les Combes.

Another strong memory here is the time when there was a massive pile up at the start in 1998 and I was doing on the spot reports for ITV F1. I realised that it was going to be a long afternoon, so I popped into a portaloo. Out of the blue Murray Walker threw to me, so I had to hurriedly retrieve my mike and make something up on the spot.

I'm looking forward to this race. Ross was saying on the plane this morning that they just need to get the tyres up to temperature and they will be competitive, but in trying to make that happen in the past by loading up corners of the car, they've introduced imbalances. He's hoping that it will work this weekend. Red Bull should be quick, although they are going to be concerned about engines for this race and the next one at Monza after Sebastian Vettel lost his fourth of the season in Valencia.

Mark Webber needs a strong weekend and preferably a win. If he doesn't win and take a big bite out of Jenson Button's lead, then it's going to make it hard with the races we have coming up.

On the tittle-tattle front, it looks as if Williams is moving closer to using Renault engines next year. And all routes seem to point to Nico Hulkenberg getting promoted to a race seat next year, possibly along-side Robert Kubica or Rubens Barrichello.

Red Bull appear to be divided on switching to Mercedes. I hear that some of the team want to do it, but there is some resistance from some key people.

* * *

Jenson Button was making heavy weather of winning the world title. After a dominant first half of the season, he lost his way in the second half as other teams and drivers became stronger. But there seemed to be a psychological dimension to it as well. Button seemed to be gripped with a fear of losing the title. Despite a relaxed veneer, beneath the surface he was clearly suffering.

* * *

Button loses his rag over question of will to win
28 August 2009

Jenson Button lost his cool yesterday with the man from *The Times*, Ed Gorman, when he suggested that in the eyes of some, Button didn't actually seem to want to win the world championship.

"I don't think people are saying that seriously! Who could possibly say that?" exploded an incredulous Button.

Button has made heavy going of closing out this world title lately, especially in Valencia where he failed to convert a winning car into a winning result. He made a mistake in qualifying and then got boxed in at the start, dropping from fifth to ninth on the opening lap. This has led to questions about whether Button has the killer instinct, that raw desire to finish off the opposition.

Button went on angrily: "'Does Jenson want this title or not?' It's a pretty silly question, isn't it? Why the f*** am I here? That is not really a proper question, is it?" he said. "In reality, that is not the right question – it can't be. 'Does he want the title?' 'No, I want to finish second or third'... "

This exchange took place in part two of his briefing yesterday afternoon. The first part was conducted in a good spirit with Button talking about being in the best position with a big advantage over his rivals. This time last year Lewis Hamilton left Spa with a single point advantage over Felipe Massa.

I always think that it is not the way a sportsman conducts himself in planned situations which counts, but how he reacts to unexpected situations. Button's hair-trigger temper yesterday, when he should have just laughed and risen above it, shows that he is clearly feeling the pressure. It *was* a pretty daft question, but a cunning one in that it produced an extreme reaction. But there is no reason to panic. The Englishman knows that there are two tracks coming up which will suit his car better than the Red Bull; Singapore and Abu Dhabi.

Raikkonen holds off Fisichella to win Spa thriller
30 August 2009

Kimi Raikkonen won the Belgian Grand Prix today, for the fourth time in his career, beating pole-sitter Giancarlo Fisichella into second place. The pair were never more than 1.1 seconds apart at any stage in a thrilling race, which turned on the restart on lap 5 after a safety car for first lap carnage.

Fisichella led through La Source but Raikkonen was able to pass him on the straight after Eau Rouge using his KERS power boost button to take a lead he would never lose. They both pitted together at each of their stops, but if Fisichella had been able to do one more lap in the second stint he would have been able to leap him. Sadly for him they were fuelled the same.

Fisichella was able to follow the Ferrari at less than a second's gap for most of the race without the tyres or the car temperatures suffering. Despite scoring Force India's best ever result (and a lucrative one, which takes them into ninth place in the constructors' championship ahead of Toro Rosso), the Italian felt that he had the faster car and Raikkonen agreed.

"He was faster," admitted Raikkonen. "We made a mistake to put on the hard tyres at the first stop. He was able to push harder but we kept him behind in the pit stops so it was hard for him to get past. I used the KERS to pass him at the restart and it was easy."

"I could have won because I was quicker than him," said Fisichella. "But anyway second is a really good result, the car was really good, I was really impressed with the pace and I hope it stays like that."

Sebastian Vettel finished third after starting in eighth position. He fought hard to pass cars through the pit stops and tracked down Robert Kubica before jumping him at the second stops for his podium place.

The start of the race saw a pile-up which was triggered by Raikkonen going off track and rejoining into the path of Jarno Trulli. Grosjean rammed Button, while Hamilton and Alguersuari collided too.

Jenson Button scored no points for the first time this season, but the damage to his championship lead was minimal, as Barrichello took only two points off him to move to 16 behind, while Vettel narrowed his deficit from 25 to 19 points.

Before the race RAI TV said that Fisichella was going to be appointed the second driver for Ferrari at Monza and the rumour has gained strength all weekend as Fisichella's results improved. Asked what he thought about the possibility of being team-mates with Fisichella at Monza, Raikkonen said, "It doesn't matter who's in the second car, it's not my decision."

BELGIAN GRAND PRIX
Spa Francorchamps 44 laps

1. Raikkonen	Ferrari		1h23:50.995
2. Fisichella	Force India-Mercedes	+	0.939
3. Vettel	Red Bull-Renault	+	3.875
4. Kubica	BMW Sauber	+	9.966
5. Heidfeld	BMW Sauber	+	11.276
6. Kovalainen	McLaren-Mercedes	+	32.763
7. Barrichello	Brawn-Mercedes	+	35.461
8. Rosberg	Williams-Toyota	+	36.208

DRIVERS' STANDINGS
1. Button   72
2. Barrichello 56
3. Vettel   53
4. Webber   51.5
5. Raikkonen   34
6. Rosberg   30.5

CONSTRUCTORS' STANDINGS
1. Brawn-Mercedes   128
2. Red Bull-Renault   104.5
3. Ferrari   56
4. McLaren-Mercedes   44
5. Toyota   38.5
6. Williams-Toyota   30.5

Chapter Nine
September 2009

September was another turbulent month for the sport. It was the month when the FIA uncovered the extraordinary plot by Renault team management to fix the result of the previous year's Singapore Grand Prix. After the turmoil of the summer it was the last thing F1 needed.

This was the worst cheating scandal to hit the sport in living memory and it led to the departure of two major figures: Flavio Briatore and Pat Symonds. Renault didn't contest the charges, but while their approach paid off in the sense that they escaped with only a suspended ban, the scandal resulted in an exodus of sponsors in the most humiliating way. Perhaps the most unsavoury aspect of the affair was the immunity granted to Nelson Piquet Junior, the very person who actually crashed the car.

Meanwhile the embarrassing episode of Luca Badoer's tenure as a Ferrari race driver came to an end with the team's announcement that Giancarlo Fisichella had been transferred from Force India.

* * *

Why a fired-up Fisichella is the right choice for Ferrari
3 September 2009

Ferrari has decided to put its faith in Giancarlo Fisichella for the remainder of the season, replacing Luca Badoer.

It is an ideal scenario for the 36-year-old from Rome, who has been in Formula 1 since 1996. He has tried before to get involved with Ferrari, but this cameo appearance of five races at the end of the season will give him a chance to live the dream and drive a Ferrari at Monza next week.

"I'm in seventh heaven," Fisichella said on the Ferrari website. "I still can't believe it - that the dream of my life comes true, and I want to thank Ferrari and chairman Luca di Montezemolo.

"Over the last week some really incredible things happened to me: the pole position and then second place at Spa and now I'm called by Ferrari to race the last five races of the season for them.

"I'll give my best to recompense the Scuderia for this great opportunity they gave me: I know that it won't be easy, but I'll give it everything to gain the best possible results."

With the news that the injured Felipe Massa is out for the rest of the season and the McLaren team threatening Ferrari's fourth place in the championship, the management at Ferrari knew that they had to go for a driver who could give them the maximum points return from his five races in the car. Ferrari has had one of their drivers on the podium in each of the last four races. But former test driver Luca Badoer was so far off the pace in Valencia and Spa that it was clear that points would be a remote possibility for him rather than a probability. In addition it was harming the Ferrari brand to have one of its cars at the back of the field, especially when the other car was winning.

It was vital for Ferrari to have a driver who was capable of scoring points straight away and one who would not have his head turned by being behind the wheel of a Ferrari at Monza.

There were some rumours that Robert Kubica might take the seat, rumours that have emanated from Italy in the last few days, but these may well have been part of a negotiating ploy, as Force India boss Vijay Mallya was hinting that he might play hardball and not release Fisichella. Kubica's size and weight were a factor though, as the Ferrari has a heavy KERS system and therefore needs a light driver.

Fisichella's is a romantic tale; the driver in the last stages of his career finally getting the call from the Scuderia after over a decade of waiting, but Fisi knows that he has an important job to do - to back up Raikkonen and keep Ferrari ahead of McLaren in the points race. They currently have a 12-point lead.

"We have chosen Fisichella because we can expect him to make a valuable contribution in this final part of the season," commented Stefano Domenicali. "Giancarlo has shown, throughout his long career, that he is fast and competitive and we are therefore proud to be able to run an Italian driver in our home race. We wish to thank Luca Badoer for the team spirit he demonstrated in these circumstances: it is a shame he was unable to show his true worth in these last two races, tackled under conditions which anyone would have found difficult."

It's debatable whether Fisi has been able to show his true worth during a 14-year career in the sport. From 223 Grands Prix he has won only three times and had four pole positions.

He is a driver who needs motivation; if his team-mate is battering him or his car is uncompetitive he can be quite anonymous, but when the car gives him a chance, as the Force India did in Spa, or when he is fired up, he is usually ready to take it. He will be supremely motivated for his spell at Ferrari.

His face will fit at Ferrari, not least because he has already worked with Massa's race engineer, Rob Smedley, during his second stint at Jordan in 2002-03, which included his victory at the crash-fest 2003 Brazilian Grand Prix. (Ironically Raikkonen was originally awarded the win, but following an appeal by Jordan the win was rightly given to Fisichella.)

Added to that, Fisi's manager, Enrico Zanarini, knows the ropes at Ferrari as he was previously Eddie Irvine's manager. It's a great story and it will provide the Italian with the perfect exit from the sport. He also becomes reserve driver for 2010... in place of Badoer.

Vatanen on potential collision course with Ecclestone?
5 September 2009

The battle to be elected FIA president is hotting up and former rally champion Ari Vatanen has seen his campaign gathering traction lately. But some of his statements indicate that, if elected, he could be on a collision course with Bernie Ecclestone and CVC, not least because of his views on the 100-year agreement between the FIA and FOM and on the circuits that Grands Prix visit.

Vatanen was in London yesterday to meet with some of the British media and I was invited along. The somewhat bizarre meeting place was the London Eye, with Vatanen conducting his press briefings in one of the slowly rotating pods. Perhaps the surroundings did give him the metaphor of far-reaching vision and total transparency that he is claiming his presidency would bring to the FIA.

Being in a pod had the effect of restricting each briefing to 30 minutes, as that is how long the pod takes to complete a circuit. The problem with that was that he tends to give very long answers so it's hard to cover much ground. But I did manage to extract some interesting stuff out of him, as did some others.

Vatanen is confident that he can beat former Ferrari boss Jean Todt in the election on 23 October. Although Todt's team has published reams of votes of support from car clubs all over the world, Vatanen claims to have greater support on the mobility side (i.e. the non-racing side) and has recently gained some strong support in the Middle East and in Japan.

His most recent success was the decision of Prince Feisal of Jordan to back him, which apparently could change the dynamic in the Middle East, a key voting region. Todt's team seem quite calm at this stage and confident that their man will prevail.

Vatanen has spent 10 years as a member of the European Parliament and done extensive work on mobility - getting people out and about. This is his primary focus, although the high profile bit of the job is Formula 1. This is also where the money comes from and I asked him whether he would want to review the 100-year deal agreed in 2001 between the FIA and Ecclestone, whereby FOM gets the commercial rights to F1 for 100 years in exchange for $350 million, less than half what the rights recoup for FOM and its partner CVC in one year.

Vatanen said, "It speaks volumes. Let's look at two figures; the $100 million fine (for McLaren in 2007) and then the global rights are $350 million. Both figures are totally disproportionate. It speaks about how the situation in the FIA is not normal at all. I don't know if it could be done [to review the deal]. Those figures are way out and they couldn't happen in a normal structure, like we are proposing."

Vatanen also spoke about pushing to keep the Formula 1 races in the traditional venues, like the UK, France and Germany, who are struggling to pay the circuit fees, rather than go to new venues which can pay higher fees, but not fill the grandstands.

"I am in favour of course of some new races - the Singapore night race or anything like that - because we need to renew ourselves.

"But if we go to the places where the stands are empty and at the same time traditional fans of F1 don't have a race, there's something wrong.

"The fact that Silverstone may not have a race, Hockenheim may not have a race next year, France may not have a race... it means we are alienating the traditional customers and fans and it is not so easy to win them back," said Vatanen.

This view will clash with those of Ecclestone and CVC who project 10 per cent growth every year in circuit fees in their business plan.

Vatanen doesn't answer questions like a politician. He seems to launch straight into his reply and then reverse his way out of a particular point if he feels he might be saying something wrong. But there is no doubting his passion and his desire to reform an old institution to serve and mobilise a far wider community in the 21st century.

Explosive new information on Renault pre-crash meeting
9 September 2009

The *Autosport* website is carrying a story this evening containing some amazing revelations about a meeting which took place between Renault's Flavio Briatore, Pat Symonds and Nelson Piquet Jr at Singapore last year.

Renault stand accused of deliberately causing Piquet to crash, just after Alonso's early first pit stop, in order to give Alonso the chance to win the race, as the rest of the field would pit under the ensuing safety car.

It appears that Nelson Piquet Jr has submitted written evidence that he was asked by Briatore and Symonds to crash his car deliberately. He says that he went through with it because he felt insecure about his contract for 2009 and Briatore was making his life uncomfortable.

Piquet claims that Symonds showed him on a map the precise location where he wanted him to crash, where there was no crane to shift the wreckage, so the race director would be forced to deploy a safety car.

Autosport says that the information was given to FIA president Max Mosley by Nelson Piquet Sr on 26 July. This was the day of the Hungarian Grand Prix. That same day Renault were charged with releasing Alonso's unsafe car back into the race after a pit stop. That infringement initially resulted in a one-race ban, which was lifted on appeal, but it planted the notion that the team had not been acting safely.

Since then the Singapore issue has been extensively investigated by an FIA team, assisted by representatives of Quest, a leading independent investigative firm. (Incidentally the firm is run by former Metropolitan police chief Lord Stevens, and it was hired by Mosley last year to look into who set up the sting on him in the *News of the World*.)

This allegation against Renault is an extremely serious one, and, if proven, is far more serious than the McLaren spy case of 2007 because it concerns putting the lives of the driver, the marshals and potentially the public at risk. If proven, the race-fixing aspect of it would have a very negative impact on the image of the sport, just as it is emerging from the instability of the teams' breakaway threat.

According to the story, both Symonds and Briatore deny Piquet's account. They accept that a meeting took place, but say that the idea of crashing was not theirs – the word of two men against one.

Interestingly, in the evidence that has come to light thus far, there is no suggestion that Fernando Alonso, who was the main beneficiary of Piquet's accident and who is hoping to be unveiled as a Ferrari driver shortly, had any part in the planning of it.

The hearing before the World Council will take place on Monday 21 September.

* * *

In the days that followed, Renault issued legal proceedings against the Piquets, father and son, for defamation and blackmail. Mosley confirmed that Piquet had been granted immunity from penalty in return for his sworn evidence and said that the FIA considers this allegation to be more serious than cheating and that the team could be thrown out of F1 altogether if found guilty. Piquet's immunity played very badly within F1 circles.

* * *

Barrichello masterpiece beats Button in Monza
13 September 2009

Rubens Barrichello took his second victory in three races at the Italian Grand Prix, heading home team-mate Jenson Button. A beautifully judged performance all weekend from the 37-year-old Brazilian put his team-mate in the shade. Whereas Button hit the ground running at the start of the season, since Turkey it has been all Barrichello.

Today was Barrichello's third win at Monza and the first time that he has headed Button in a Brawn 1-2 finish. His performance took him to only 14 points behind Button in the championship and with the Red Bull pair of Mark Webber and Sebastian Vettel pretty much out of it now, it looks very much as if the title fight will be between the Brawn drivers. It is also possible that the team will clinch the constructors' championship before the end of the season, perhaps in Japan.

The Brawn pair started the race in 5th and 6th places on the grid, but made the most of a one-stop strategy to come through and pass pole-sitter Lewis Hamilton as well as Kimi Raikkonen and Adrian Sutil, all of whom two-stopped. Hamilton was set for a third place, but crashed on the last lap while pushing hard to catch Button. This gave Raikkonen a podium.

Adrian Sutil scored his first points in F1 with fourth place, but it could have been third had Sutil not hit one of his mechanics on his second stop, losing some time in the process. He set the fastest lap, but spent the whole race behind the Ferrari of Raikkonen, who again drove a canny race using all his skill and guile - not to mention his KERS button - to keep the faster car at bay.

Barrichello won the race by having the edge over Button on pace when it mattered in qualifying and by his consistency in the race itself. He also survived a gearbox worry before the race. He made an excellent start to pass Kovalainen and move up to fourth place.

He had an extra lap of fuel compared to Button, and also he made a decision to start the race on the hard tyre, whereas Button started on soft. Both tyres worked well on the Brawn, but it meant that Barrichello had better pace immediately after the pit stops and was able to open up a margin over Button.

Ross Brawn was delighted with his fourth 1-2 finish of the season and says that he doesn't mind which of his drivers wins the world title from here. "I demand they do it fairly and openly, everything has got to be fair and open. We will leave them to it. They are old enough," he said.

"Jenson was beating him (Rubens) consistently at the start of the season but Valencia was a great race for Rubens and he has a steely look about him at the moment."

Hamilton looked good in the early stages, but his ability to open up a big enough gap to cover the Brawns fell apart in the middle stint. By the time he pitted for the second time on lap 35 he was nothing like far enough ahead and the Brawns jumped him.

Heikki Kovalainen had a disappointing day. I posted yesterday that he should win the race, based on his car pace and his strategy and grid slot. He had a similar strategy to the Brawns and started ahead of them on the grid. But he lost ground at the start and faded off the pace. At the end he was 60 seconds behind Barrichello and was 57 seconds behind Hamilton on the last lap.

Team boss Martin Whitmarsh recently put the spotlight on Kovalainen's wavering race pace and today will have been a hammer blow to the Finn's hopes of retaining his seat. He simply should have done a lot better.

ITALIAN GRAND PRIX
Monza 53 laps

1. Barrichello	Brawn-Mercedes	(1h16:21.706
2. Button	Brawn-Mercedes	+ 2.866
3. Raikkonen	Ferrari	+ 30.664
4. Sutil	Force India-Merc	+ 31.131
5. Alonso	Renault	+ 59.182
6. Kovalainen	McLaren-Mercedes	+ 1:00.693
7. Heidfeld	BMW Sauber	+ 1:22.412
8. Vettel	Red Bull-Renault	+ 1:25.427

DRIVERS' STANDINGS
1. Button	80	
2. Barrichello	66	.
3. Vettel	54	
4. Webber	51.5	
5. Raikkonen	40	
6. Rosberg	30	

CONSTRUCTORS' STANDINGS
1. Brawn-Mercedes	146
2. Red Bull-Renault	105.5
3. Ferrari	62
4. McLaren-Mercedes	47
5. Toyota	38.5
6. Williams-Toyota	30.5

Barrichello's a winner whatever happens from here on 13 September 2009

Rubens Barrichello was magnificent this weekend at the Italian Grand Prix. Whatever happens from now on, whether he is able to beat Jenson Button to the world championship or not, the whole season has been a win for him.

He didn't have a drive in January and yet his stunning performances in the second half of the season, including two wins, have done more than enough to cement his place in F1 next year, for an unprecedented 18th season! As Ross Brawn said to me recently, he sees no reason why he wouldn't retain Barrichello for next year.

Of course, since he said that he appears to have agreed to sell a controlling interest in the team to Mercedes and there are suggestions that they would like to have a German driver in the car, possibly Rosberg.

But even in that eventuality, Rubens has shown that he is still capable of sitting at F1's top table and Williams and several others would have him in a heartbeat. His maturity combined with his enduring passion for the sport means that he is able to calmly put together complete race weekends one after another. Not too many drivers in F1 can do that. He is also as good as anyone out there technically, especially at setting a car up.

His Achilles' heel is braking; he has to have a car with good braking stability and suffers if he doesn't get it. Luckily for him the Brawn is very strong in that area.

Looking at him this weekend without his beard he looked younger than ever, rejuvenated by a competitive season and by his ability to get the best from himself and his car. Barrichello is on target to make a real piece of history; he is already the most experienced driver by far with 279 starts and that means next year, if the calendar has 18 races as we believe it will, he'll break the 300 Grand Prix starts barrier before the end of the 2010 season!

"I think it is a winning year whatever happens," said Barrichello this afternoon. "We have got to remember that it is not long ago we had no jobs. We did not know what is going to happen, so we are finally driving a fantastic car with a fantastic engine. The team are doing a fantastic job. I must thank them for all of their efforts."

* * *

A few days after Monza, F1 was heading for another appointment at the World Council in Paris. The shock waves produced by the Renault Singapore race-fixing scandal reverberated widely. F1 and its credibility were on trial. At the epicentre was Pat Symonds, who was faced with a tough decision; to accept immunity in return for burying his long-time ally Flavio Briatore, or stand solid with his boss and face a potentially career-ending ban.

* * *

A very difficult moment for Renault's Pat Symonds
15 September 2009

Who would want to swap places with Renault's director of engineering, Pat Symonds? The veteran, whose F1 career goes back almost 30 years to the Toleman team, is the only engineer to have worked with Senna, Schumacher and Alonso and is always fascinating on the subject of motor sport.

It has been a career of great distinction. He hasn't worked for Ferrari, Williams or McLaren but he has twice helped a new team break their stranglehold on F1 success, with Benetton in the 1990s and Renault in the 2000s. Both phases brought double world championships and although there was a whiff of controversy about some of the technical aspects of the 1990s successes with Benetton, no one in F1 would deny that Pat is one of the good guys and a very well respected engineer and strategist. Many people in F1 are totally shocked at his involvement in this plot.

Symonds's successes have all come in partnership with Flavio Briatore and the two have a very strong relationship, but now Symonds has been offered the chance to save himself and his career by telling "the truth" about what happened in Singapore in 2008 over Nelson Piquet's crash. Piquet has already been given immunity by the FIA in return for spilling the beans and that same privilege has now been extended to

Symonds. The FIA feel that he has a lot more to tell them than he has so far and may be more willing to do so in return for a deal.

Judging from the transcript below, Symonds was being very cagey when he met the FIA investigators at Spa. But as more and more evidence emerges into the media ahead of the hearing next Monday (21 September), Symonds has to make a very difficult decision: to risk his career and his reputation or to drop Briatore in it.

Of course if it transpires that everything happened exactly as Piquet alleges, with Symonds suggesting the accident and showing Piquet when and where to crash to guarantee a safety car, then Symonds's reputation will take a serious enough knock to end his career anyway.

The radio transcripts from the period around the crash are released in *The Times* newspaper today. They are interesting but not conclusive. So far the only weighty evidence has come from Piquet himself. But that is one man's word against that of two others. Symonds has already said that the suggestion of crashing was Piquet's and was made the day before the race. He does not however confirm or deny whether the discussion on Sunday covered this subject, so he has left himself room to confirm everything Piquet alleges, if indeed that is how things transpired.

This is a real life, high stakes drama of the kind dreamt up by Hollywood script writers. It shows why movies about F1 are pointless: because the real thing is more than dramatic enough already.

Here are some extracts from the transcript of the FIA interview with Symonds:

FIA adviser: In your own words Mr Symonds what do you recall being said to Nelson Piquet Jr at that meeting? This is shortly before the race.

Symonds: I don't really remember it.

FIA adviser: You don't remember?

Symonds: No.

FIA adviser: Nelson Piquet Jr says that he was asked by you to cause a deliberate crash. Is that true?

Symonds: Nelson had spoken to me the day before and suggested that. That's all I'd really like to say.

FIA adviser: Mr Symonds were you aware that there was going to be a crash at Lap 14?

Symonds: I don't want to answer that question.

FIA adviser: Mr Piquet Jr also says at that meeting you pointed out a specific place on the circuit where he was to have the accident and said it was because it was the furthest away from any of the safety or lifting equipment and gave the most likely chance of a safety car being deployed.

Symonds: I don't, I don't want to answer that question.

FIA adviser: [Referring to the pre-race meeting] Was it you that did the talking at that meeting Mr Symonds?

Symonds: I'm sure it would have been both of us but I don't know for sure. Sorry that's a contradiction. I would imagine it would be both of us that would be normal. Actually probably more often it's Flavio that does the talking himself. I wouldn't necessarily always agree with what he's saying but the majority.

FIA adviser: Can I say that if Mr Symonds you'd been put in the position where you were made to ask Mr Piquet Jr to crash, it would be much better for you in the long term to tell these stewards to hear that today?

Symonds: I fully understand that.

FIA adviser: Yes.

Symonds: I have no intention of lying to you. I have not lied to you but I have reserved my position just a little.

FIA adviser: And you're aware that the stewards may draw conclusions from your unwillingness to assist them in relation to what went on in that meeting?

Symonds: I would expect them to. I would absolutely expect that.

The rights and wrongs of immunity
15 September 2009

I'm interested in the rights and wrongs of the FIA offering immunity from prosecution to Nelson Piquet Jr and Pat Symonds - but not to Flavio Briatore - in the Singapore crash investigation.

I spoke to a London litigation lawyer this evening and he said that the key points here are:

> i) this is not a case in the criminal courts, where, in the UK at least, plea bargaining is not really done. It is subject to the rules of the FIA. I don't know what those rules are with regard to disciplinary hearings and whether the FIA has the right to offer plea bargains;
>
> ii) were the FIA on to something already when Piquet gave his evidence, in other words did he go to them or did they quiz him first? The story we've seen so far seems to suggest that the Piquets started this particular ball rolling, in other words the FIA was alerted by them. As for offering Symonds immunity, is this offer intended to get at the truth generally, or is it designed specifically to incriminate Briatore - i.e. on what terms has Pat been offered immunity?

Earlier today I asked one of *JA on F1's* regular readers, Harveyeight, who is an ex-CID policeman, to give me his views on the whys and wherefores of an immunity offer. He has been involved in a lot of investigations and interviews of suspects in the real world and is also clearly passionate about F1 so I was interested in his view. Here it is:

"My instinct is to say that if you can't trust anyone to tell the truth without inducements you can't trust them to tell the truth.

"The FIA do not have to prove their case beyond a reasonable doubt, as explained by Werewolf [another blogger]. So we have the threshold of the balance of probabilities. If you can't reach that without some kind of prepayment then your case must be pretty weak.

"Further, the FIA has protection against a duff decision built in to the law. To go into Pope mode and grant forgiveness of sins without repentance seems an abuse of the protection.

"The penalty for Flav, the sponsors, Renault itself and, as you pointed out, the Renault workers, is severe. The decision must be 100 per cent certain. Anything else is a betrayal of the FIA's responsibility. The innocent victims in all of this cannot be seen as collateral damage.

"Further, and this is a personal moral stance I know, ignoring all the political implications which the FIA must have cognisance of, if three people have conspired then they should all be punished.

"Many people have suffered in this matter already. Heaven knows what is going through the minds of the team workers and their families. How will they feel after, perhaps, losing their houses, their kids education, their holidays and their security to see Piquet walk free and back to his life of indulgent luxury? SBS CEO anyone?

"I know life is not fair but the FIA have treated Piquet as some kind of hero for, if he is to be believed, keeping shtum about the incident for 12 months and then, when galvanised into action by his sacking, eventually got daddy to go to the FIA. Some hero. But some reward, eh?

"My personal experience of those offered some kind of deal – never immunity at my level – is that they remain selective in their memory. Informants are one thing, co-conspirators are another. My belief always was that they started lying for their mates and ended up lying against them. Either way, not to be trusted.

"You suggest in your question that they are being given immunity for the truth. That's not quite correct. They are being given immunity for saying what the prosecution wants to hear. A difference, and not a subtle one. Piquet is not an insider, giving evidence against those for whom he worked. This is against, if he is to be believed, those who conspired with him.

"So to be rather Micawberish, in short I don't trust evidence gained by absolution. But, as importantly, if Piquet and Pat have conspired, they should be punished. And severely."

Why Mercedes is moving towards Brawn, away from McLaren
19 September 2009

Amid all the furore over the Renault race-fixing scandal, this week has seen another important development in shaping the next generation of F1.

I posted last week on the news that Mercedes was set to take a controlling interest in the Brawn team. It appears that the deal has been worked with the backing of the Abu Dhabi investment vehicle Aabar, which bought 9.1 per cent of the Mercedes parent company, Daimler, earlier this year. It is the company's largest shareholder.

Aabar is an interesting company with a wide range of investments in many different sectors. They bought a 32 per cent stake in Virgin Galactic, Sir Richard Branson's space project recently.

According to *Auto Motor und Sport's* Michael Schmidt, who is usually pretty good on these matters, the Mercedes shareholding in the Brawn team will be held by Aabar until the end of 2011, at which point clauses in Mercedes' contract with McLaren lapse and allow them to take equity in another team.

The suggestion is, however, that from next year onwards the Brawn car will carry more significant Mercedes branding, the three-pointed star on the engine cover and so on. There is also a strong suggestion that Nico Rosberg will drive there. One would expect Jenson Button to partner him, but the championship leader is being squeezed in negotiations over a new deal at the moment. With a much bigger picture in play now at Brawn, he may opt to stay with what is clearly a team of the future and settle for what's on the table.

Brawn is known to have signed a title sponsor and two secondary sponsors for next season. There are others negotiating the remaining positions on the car and the Mercedes involvement will attract others.

The team are keeping the details close to their chests, but I have heard a suggestion that one of the secondary sponsors may be Orange, the mobile phone giant. It seems that another may be a Germany company as well as one from the Far East. It is known that LG is interested in sponsoring a team next season, in addition to its extensive spend with Bernie Ecclestone and FOM thus far, but I have not heard of any direct connection with Brawn yet.

Meanwhile Mercedes continue to own a 40 per cent stake in McLaren. A further 30 per cent is owned by the Bahraini investment fund. It seems that Mercedes now want to own a controlling stake in a team and have decided to go with Brawn. It is well known that Mercedes have at various times wanted to take a controlling interest in McLaren but have been unable to do so.

It is not clear yet what Mercedes would do with its 40 per cent McLaren stake, once it takes up its Brawn position, but there is no doubt that their involvement and financial contribution are amongst the most valuable assets of the McLaren team, which has a huge staff and a very expensive factory to run. So where does this leave McLaren and what has motivated Mercedes to move?

Well part of it is obviously the desire to have more control over a team. Also the recent scandals over stolen Ferrari data and lyng to the stewards have taken their toll on the relationship. In neither episode were Mercedes directly involved, but they will have suffered by association. However one of the real keys to this move lies in the supercar market. McLaren this week unveiled its MP4 12C road car, a Gullwing-door sports car, which is aimed squarely at Ferrari's market - the £120,000 to £170,000 market.

Before the credit crunch Ferrari was selling around 6,000 cars a year and all the forecasts are that this sector of the market will be buoyant again soon, offering a great opportunity. McLaren's Ron Dennis, in exile from F1, is throwing all his efforts into the development of this car which will, significantly, be powered by a McLaren engine, not a Mercedes one.

And here is the crunch, Mercedes is also targeting that sector, with its Gullwing SLS AMG, which was launched this week at Frankfurt Motor Show. McLaren is building a car which will be in direct competition with Mercedes in what is a lucrative sector.

McLaren and Mercedes worked together on the SLR, but Dennis has always had ambitions to produce the "British Ferrari". He feels that as he has beaten them on the track he can beat them in showroom sales too. It's a strategy which seems to have put the company on a collision course with Mercedes.

Speaking at the Frankfurt Motor Show this week, where the SLS was launched, Daimler boss Dr Zetsche said:

"For a long period we had a lack of alignment on road cars [with McLaren] but we have now found a clear solution and we won't participate."

As for where things go with McLaren from here in terms of F1 he added: "Ending the relationship is not an option but we may have a different relationship."

What makes this story so poignant is that the Brawn team wouldn't have existed without McLaren's support at the start of the 2009 season. Mercedes were very keen to provide a lifeline to Brawn, and a very powerful and reliable engine has been one of the cornerstones of their success - particularly in competition with Red Bull, whose Renault has lacked the power and proved a little unreliable, especially for Sebastian Vettel.

But McLaren's CEO, Martin Whitmarsh, full of the early spirit of brotherhood of FOTA, facilitated the Mercedes deal and helped the Brawn team. All of that happened in the weeks leading up to that notorious FOTA press conference in Geneva.

He clearly didn't see this situation coming.

* * *

After Renault's decision not to contest the disrepute charge for its part in the Singapore race fixing scandal, it was always likely that Flavio Briatore would be the fall guy. But it was still a shock when the FIA World Council handed down a lifetime ban.

* * *

Briatore banned for life, Renault escape lightly
21 September 2009

Flavio Briatore has been banned from motor sport for life and his co-conspirator Pat Symonds for five years, but Renault itself escaped lightly, with a two-year suspended ban and no fine for the Singapore crash scandal.

The hearing in Paris today took just 90 minutes and was attended by Renault Sport president Bernard Rey, Fernando Alonso and Nelson Piquet.

As expected Briatore came off worst today, the World Motor Sport Council taking a very dim view of the fact that he continued to deny any involvement in the plot, despite the FIA's and Renault's own investigations concluding that he was involved, albeit that the FIA were not as comprehensively convinced as Renault.

The result is a ban which not only means that he is expressly forbidden to attend F1 races again, but also GP2 races (of which he is the founder) and in addition he must decouple himself from the driver management company which looks after Mark Webber, Heikki Kovalainen and others, or the drivers will not receive superlicences, without which they cannot race. His lieutenants, the Michel brothers, will probably take over but it remains to be seen whether the allure of being managed by them without Briatore's influence behind the scenes is attractive to the drivers.

Pat Symonds was given a five-year ban because he admitted his part in the conspiracy and also wrote a submission to the WMSC that it was to his "eternal regret and shame" that he participated in it. He will be 62 at the end of the ban and may not return to the sport at all, on that basis.

Renault had already decided not to contest the charges so it was down to Rey to submit some mitigating pleas. He offered to pay the FIA's costs of the investigation and to contribute funds to FIA road safety campaigns. That did the trick, with the WMSC deciding not only to suspend Renault's ban for two years, but to activate it only if the team commits a "comparable" crime again, which is highly unlikely.

Briatore's scalp was always the main target for the FIA, but Renault's punishment will still look rather odd in the history books compared to the huge fine McLaren got two years ago for a far less serious offence. The difference between the two in the FIA's eyes appears to be honesty, in the way the team conducted itself once the plot was uncovered and tackled its defence of the charges. But $100 million is an awful lot of honesty in comparison with the sheer danger involved with Renault's transgression.

According to the FIA statement, "Renault F1 stated at the meeting that it had conducted a detailed internal investigation, which found that: (i) Flavio Briatore, Pat Symonds and Nelson Piquet Jr had conspired to cause the crash; and (ii) no other team member was involved in the conspiracy."

Most controversially, Nelson Piquet walks away scot-free, despite having been one of the three conspirators, because he was granted immunity at the outset, in exchange for the information; this will play badly with many in the sport.

Fernando Alonso was cleared of any involvement.

* * *

Pat Symonds's letter to the WMSC was published shortly after the verdict. He maintained his position that the idea was first suggested by Nelson Piquet and went on, "In a single action I have destroyed the high reputation I have built up during a 33-year career in motor sport. I am a competitive person who worked in a high pressure environment. This can, at times, cloud one's judgement. I have always tried to be an honest person, a fact I hope you will give me credit for by witness of my statements to the stewards in Belgium. On that night in Singapore last year I made a mistake the consequences of which I could never have imagined at the time. For that mistake I can only offer all of you, and all those touched by the action I was involved in, my profound apology."

* * *

Piquet: "Sorry about that, now who wants to hire me?" 21 September 2009

Nelson Piquet Jr issued a statement today, after the World Motor Sport Council verdict was announced, which again slammed his former team boss Flavio Briatore, much as he had done in the summer after being sacked.

I find it incredibly ironic that a season, which began with Briatore saying some extremely uncomplimentary things about Jenson Button, referring to him as a "concrete post" has ended up concluding with Briatore himself being derided on all sides and hammered by one of his drivers. Flavio is the classic example of the old saying, "You live by the sword, you die by the sword."

He has made a fortune from motor sport and many other businesses, so his life and livelihood are not ruined. He will suffer some associated difficulties with Queens Park Rangers as he could be disqualified from holding more than 30 per cent of the shares as a result of his F1 ban. But the real pain he will be suffering is the double whammy of Piquet hanging him out to dry and Max Mosley using this as an opportunity to finish him off as a player in F1.

Piquet says that while he regrets his actions, it's all over now and he's keen to show one of the F1 teams what he can really do.

He claims that many drivers have suffered what he suffered at Briatore's hands; the uncertainty over their futures, being treated as a commodity and discarded at will. Piquet, having found himself on the scrap heap at 23 decided not to take it lying down, but to take a stand and that is what led to the Singapore scandal seeing the light of day.

Piquet's father, Nelson Sr revealed an unfortunate truth this week when he said that he told the FIA's Charlie Whiting what his son had done in October 2008. The FIA has tried to brush that under the carpet, saying that it was up to his son to make a sworn statement in order to launch an enquiry and that is what they did second time around in July 2009.

"I am relieved that the FIA investigation has now been concluded," Piquet Jr said. "Those now running the Renault F1 Team took the decision, as I did, that it is better that the truth be known and accept the consequences. The most positive thing to come from bringing this to the attention of the FIA is that nothing like it will ever happen again.

"I bitterly regret my actions to follow the orders I was given. I wish every day that I had not done it."

* * *

Shortly after the verdict was announced, the FIA released details about some evidence which had turned the course of the enquiry; the testimony of mysterious "Witness X". This provoked feverish speculation as to the identity of this witness.

Many people believed it was Fernando Alonso. Personally I think it was more likely to be an engineer. According to the FIA, "When the FIA's advisers interviewed Witness X, he expressly confirmed that Mr Briatore was involved in the conspiracy because Witness X had been personally present at a meeting shortly after qualifying on Saturday 27 September 2008 when Mr Symonds had mentioned the possibility of a crash plan to Mr Briatore. The FIA's advisers were confident that Witness X himself played no active role in the conspiracy."

After a period of reflection, Briatore launched a lawsuit in the French courts to try to overturn the ban.

As soon as the Renault case was put to bed, things started moving quickly in the saga of Fernando Alonso's move to Ferrari. There was no evidence of Alonso being implicated in the "fix", but Ferrari saw an opportunity to make a move.

* * *

Ferrari driver situation "has changed"
25 September 2009

Things are moving quickly now in the one key move in the driver market which will unlock the others. Today Ferrari boss Stefano Domenicali said, "In the last couple of days the situation has changed, so we will keep you updated as soon as we can say something. At the moment nothing to add on that."

What did he mean?

Ferrari president Luca di Montezemolo was in Madrid on Thursday and took part in a question and answer session with the readers of *Marca*, the leading daily sports paper. He was collecting one of their awards. He allowed himself to get a bit carried away, as he does sometimes, and said the following:

"I'm happy with the five year deal with Bank Santander. I'm happy to have a Spanish sponsor and I'm pleased with my team with Alonso." But he was toying with them because he then said, "Next year we will have Massa, Raikkonen and a Spanish sponsor."

It was almost as if he was enjoying the moment, the speculation, and encouraging it. However he did then get serious and lay out the plan.

"Up to now the priority was to confirm Massa was okay in himself. Then we needed to get some certainty he would be okay as a driver. We've got that and Felipe will be with us. In these last few days we have cleared up a few things and when Domenicali returns from Singapore we can decide some important things. All the great drivers have passed through Ferrari apart from Clark, Stewart and Senna. I consider Alonso a great driver."

So it seems we are possibly a week or so away from knowing whether the Alonso Ferrari move is on or not, nine months after it was first mooted in *Gazzetta dello Sport*.

What has changed? Perhaps on his visit to Spain, Montezemolo got some kind of assurance from Santander that they would be willing to put up the extra funds needed to facilitate the early transfer of Alonso to Ferrari in place of Raikkonen.

Perhaps Alonso is now keen to distance himself from Renault and the cheating scandal, just as Michael Schumacher was in 1995, with the same team when it was Benetton. The parallels between Alonso's career and Schumacher's are amazing - both had early opportunities with Flavio Briatore's team, both won back-to-back titles then had a fallow period. Maybe the pattern continues with the move to Ferrari.

Raikkonen said on Thursday, "I believe that they want to speak to me about this. But it hasn't happened yet." Indeed, Italian colleagues tell me that Raikkonen has been seeking a meeting with Montezemolo but has yet to get a date from him. His name continues to be linked with McLaren but the team denied that there was a pre-contract in place.

As for Massa, Domenicali gave an update on his condition today. "Felipe makes steady progress: he has started a programme of physical exercise and preparations to drive. The next step will be the simulator and then he can drive a kart. When he can get back behind the wheel of a Formula 1 single-seater, we'll decide when the next steps have been completed."

A final note on Montezemolo. He was asked whether he felt he was "Mosley's next victim", following on from Flavio Briatore, the other key architect of the FOTA breakaway this summer, to which he replied, "In life you must have a clear conscience and fear nothing."

It was the kind of rich irony which only F1 can serve up; the next Grand Prix on the calendar after the Renault race fixing scandal was... the Singapore Grand Prix. Renault made some short-term management changes, promoting veteran engineer Bob Bell to the role of team principal and Jean-François Caubet to the position of managing director. Caubet gave a press briefing which was striking in its openness.

* * *

"We're walking through fire"; Renault reaction to latest setback 25 September 2009

New Renault managing director Jean-François Caubet has said that Renault has suffered immense damage to its brand and considered an F1 pull-out. It has decided to commit itself to the sport, but must put in place a management structure that will keep the team true to Renault's values.

This weekend has been utterly humiliating for the team so far, with the high profile rejection by two sponsors, ING and Mutua Madrilena. To be cast off like that by two blue chip international companies gives Renault a pariah status that is hard to comprehend for one of the world's leading car companies. It shows how the colossal media power of F1, when used as a force for bad, can cause unimaginable damage even to a great institution like Renault.

There are the inevitable rumours this weekend that the team might be sold, with the usual suspects like David Richards linked with the team, but Caubet spelt out that Renault has already gone through its self-analysis phase and decided to keep going.

"Faced with this affair we had a choice," said Caubet to the French media last night. "To stop or to walk through the fire. We decided to walk through the fire and we're coming out pretty burnt, because the image of the brand has been extremely badly damaged.

"If we had wanted to stop F1, we would have done it sooner, to spare ourselves from all of that. More than words, we are speaking through our actions. Whether it be in the development of drivers, the engine supply side or the engagement in our car for 2010, which is almost done. What is impressive is the coherence of the team. There were many tensions and they are still there, because we are asking ourselves a lot of questions; ING is leaving us, the money is difficult, what is the future of Alonso and of the business model for F1?"

As for the future management structure of the team, Renault has given itself four months to come up with the right plan. On the rumours of Alain Prost making a return to F1 as team principal of Renault, my trusted French colleagues say that he has asked for a very high salary, which isn't playing well with the Renault management.

"We've opted for a temporary (management) solution because the team is bouncing back," said Caubet. "Obviously it has gone through a painful and humiliating shock but it is working. The technical direction is under control, the drivers are determined and Viry [the engine base] is little by little rediscovering its reliability. We haven't followed up a single contact to find a team principal yet. First we need to determine the ideal profile, then find the right candidate. That could be December or January."

Caubet admitted that by giving Flavio Briatore a free rein in the management of the team, it had got too far away from Renault's brand values and ultimately ended in a hugely damaging scandal,

"This team has to rediscover the Renault culture," said Caubet. "It has lost it a bit and it will be important to rediscover it. We have to rebuild links with the Renault base and on the ethical plan renew a respectful culture towards the rules and the sporting spirit. Beyond that we need to know what will be the tools which will permit us to manage the team in an efficient manner. We don't want to fall back into the ways of the 1980s when the corporate side ran the race team, but we also do not want to reproduce the errors which have been made in leaving the team too much autonomy. We give ourselves four months to find a good compromise, the right level of autonomy."

The team has removed the ING and Mutua Madrilena stickers from its cars, but is not able to do so from the race shirts and overalls. So unless some rapid tailoring gets done, the ING executives will be unhappy to see their logos on the team personnel on the television pictures all weekend.

Interestingly the team has placed previously unseen Renault stickers on the engine cover and other bodywork areas, which means that they may have had a heads-up that they might need to bring out some stickers to replace ING's name.

Hamilton strolls to Singapore win as rivals make mistakes
27 September 2009

Lewis Hamilton won the Singapore Grand Prix with a faultless drive from pole position to redeem himself after his last lap crash in Monza. But his task was made easier by key errors from his two main rivals, Nico Rosberg and Sebastian Vettel.

Both made mistakes in pit stops which brought them drive-through penalties; Rosberg had done the hard work at the start, passing Vettel off the line to take second place, but then he got into trouble when he made a slip after his pit stop and crossed the white line on the pit exit.

Vettel was penalised for speeding in the pit lane. Rosberg was doubly unlucky as his penalty was handed out just as a safety car was deployed and it meant that he had to serve it when the field was all bunched up, which dropped him down to 14th place. Any hope of that first victory was gone.

Vettel had a little more luck. Although he lost second place through his error, his drive-through happened later on in the race and he was able to rejoin in seventh place and then pick off other cars when they made their second stops. He ended up fourth. "It's all we could do in the end. I had a chance of a podium. I was surprised when I got the call for speeding in the pit lane. It's disappointing because the car was quick."

Apart from Hamilton, the happiest man in Singapore tonight will be Jenson Button. He extended his lead over Rubens Barrichello in the points table to 15 with three races remaining, thanks to a strong recovery drive from 12th on the grid. He had quite severe brake problems at the end of the race and had to nurse the car home, but managed to finish in fifth place, one spot ahead of Barrichello. Button was helped by a call from the pits not to pit after Mark Webber had a crash. Many drivers thought that a safety car might come out so they dived into the pits, but Button stayed out, correctly as it turned out, and jumped both Heikki Kovalainen and Barrichello.

For Hamilton it was his second victory of the season and proof that he and McLaren are ending it as consistent front runners. "I came here wanting to redeem myself after the last race and I did it, " he said. "The race was straightforward for me. I built a big enough gap and was never under serious pressure. I felt it was a nicely controlled race. I had no problems in the car but the team came on the radio and said there was a fault with the KERS so I had to disable and then re-engage it but it was no problem. The focus you need here is as much as you can get, it's just corner after corner, there is no let up and it's bumpy."

Arguably the driver of the day was Toyota's Timo Glock, who equalled his best ever result in second place. He drove a perfect race, which was made by his audacious pass on Alonso at the start. His luck was really in as Mark Webber was told to let Alonso through as he had retained his position by going off the race track and in order to do that he had to let Glock through first. So Glock gained two key places.

Alonso being passed by Glock was a decisive moment because he was never able to get back on terms with the Toyota driver. Nevertheless after the two weeks Renault has just endured, it is perhaps appropriate that they should get their first podium of the season here.

"The result is great for us, first podium of the season and it was a great race," said Alonso afterwards.

Webber didn't finish the race. Clearly he had brake problems when he made his second stop, but the mechanics inspected his right front brake and sent him back out. Shortly afterwards he had a brake failure which pitched him off the circuit.

SINGAPORE GRAND PRIX
Marina Bay 61 laps

1.	Hamilton	McLaren-Mercedes		1h56:06.337
2.	Glock	Toyota	+	9.634
3.	Alonso	Renault	+	16.624
4.	Vettel	Red Bull-Renault	+	20.261
5.	Button	Brawn-Mercedes	+	30.015
6.	Barrichello	Brawn-Mercedes	+	31.858
7.	Kovalainen	McLaren-Mercedes	+	36.157
8.	Kubica	BMW Sauber	+	55.054

DRIVERS' STANDINGS
1. Button   84
2. Barrichello   69
3. Vettel   59
4. Webber   51.5
5. Raikkonen   40
6. Hamilton   37

CONSTRUCTORS' STANDINGS
1. Brawn-Mercedes   153
2. Red Bull-Renault   110.5
3. Ferrari   62
4. McLaren-Mercedes   59
5. Toyota   46.5
6. Williams-Toyota   30.5

In Singapore, Jean Todt made his first visit to a Grand Prix since becoming a candidate for the FIA presidency, unlike his rival Ari Vatanen who had attended most Grands Prix through the late summer, raising his profile and meeting the teams. Todt was keen to appear presidential. At this stage he was still the red-hot favourite in most people's eyes.

* * *

Todt steps up his bid for FIA presidency
28 September 2009

This weekend has seen a PR blitz by Jean Todt as the campaign to be elected FIA president enters the final stages. The election is less than a month away and Todt has made his first visit to the F1 paddock since announcing his candidacy.

Outgoing FIA president Max Mosley has already publicly endorsed him and this week belittled his rival, Ari Vatanen. Also this week Bernie Ecclestone came out strongly in support of Todt. This is no surprise; it was Ecclestone who persuaded Ferrari president Luca di Montezemolo to hire Todt back in 1993 when he was at Peugeot.

In everything that he has done lately Todt has striven to look presidential. He has been clever, using his status as an FIA official on the Keep Roads Safe campaign to do a series of high profile FIA-sponsored events, making it very easy for people to imagine him in the president's role. In fact he looks like he is already!

There was a fascinating little cameo on the grid on Sunday, picked up by the world feed cameras, when Todt was proceeding down the grid like a president, surrounded by people including Ecclestone, when Ari Vatanen accidentally pushed Bernie from behind as he jostled to be in on the group. You heard Bernie snap at him, "Hey, don't push". Vatanen looked like such an outsider in that group.

Thinking about it, Vatanen looks like an outsider in every sense, someone who talks a good game, but who has no direct experience of leading a large organisation. Maybe the outsider is the role he has chosen for himself, but the question is, does he have enough support? Max Mosley criticised him for never having run anything in the past, even his own rally car and it is true that it would take a leap of imagination to see him match Todt for leadership qualities. But Todt has a lot of baggage and carries the endorsement of Mosley and Ecclestone, which is a mixed blessing in the eyes of some. Vatanen represents a complete change of culture.

The key for Todt is whether he can decouple his instinct and track record of ruthless competitiveness from his broader management skills. There is no question that he is one of the great managers of sporting history, possibly the greatest in F1 in terms of results, but he pushed everything to the limit and sometimes beyond in his relentless pursuit of victory. In this new role there would be no place for that side of him, even though he would be required to fight the FIA's corner, but the sport would clearly benefit from his ability to get things done.

Would he show the face he presented to the other teams at Indianapolis in 2005, when the Michelin teams ended up not running because he would not countenance any changes to the track which might allow them to? Or would he bring the same ability to win the day to benefit the FIA and the sport as a whole?

Todt is closely aligned with Mosley and Ecclestone and although he would bring about important structural changes - such as the F1 commissioner and the disciplinary panel – which I think are excellent ideas, would he be prepared to bring about a cultural change too?

The question then is whether the key members of the FIA have the stomach for an overhaul of the way things work. If Vatanen can persuade enough of the right people to support his desire to bring about that change, he will be put in a unique and privileged position. Equally, if he can't find some game-changing moves soon, he could just be steamrollered by the Todt establishment juggernaut.

Ecclestone's endorsement is significant, even if it is slightly odd that he would come out on the side of one candidate. He usually backs a winner, though.

"I have known Jean for many years," Ecclestone said on Friday. "He is a most reliable, gifted and trustworthy person. He is determined and dedicated to whatever goals he sets himself and I admire and respect him greatly for everything he has achieved. The FIA needs a president who is strong, capable and with experience at the highest levels of motor sport. Jean is by far the most knowledgeable and capable candidate for this vitally important role. I hope everybody will support his candidacy."

Meanwhile Todt has this weekend met with the teams through FOTA and with the Grand Prix Drivers' Association. There is some concern among the FOTA hardcore about a Todt presidency and Toyota's John Howett has already expressed his view that the president should not be someone with such strong links to F1 and to one team in particular, and F1's most important team historically and financially at that.

It's interesting and significant that the two most potentially awkward team principals, as far as a Todt presidency would be concerned, have now left the sport, namely Ron Dennis and Flavio Briatore. Todt would not have been able to come in to the job and get rid of them but without them his life as president would be much easier.

Todt however hinted that some of the FIA frontline figures in F1 might be moved on.

"I am ready to start from a white sheet of paper at all levels," he said. "I will forget that I had a problem with a team because it would be inappropriate. So starting from a white piece of paper, if some people are now involved in the administration of the FIA [it's because] they are good, I can only respect them.

"If I feel that some people are not appropriate or should be put in another position it is something I will discuss with the team. And it needs to be reinforced."

The election is on 23 October.

* * *

Shortly after Singapore's race came the announcement that we had been expecting all season: Fernando Alonso was to join Ferrari on a three-year contract. Having backed my Italian colleague Pino Allievi's instinct and knowledge on this one since last December it was a great relief to see the deed finally done and made official. Essentially it amounted to the transferring out of Kimi Raikkonen, who had started performing at a very high level over the summer, and the transferring in of Alonso. I was in no doubt why this was happening; the

Spanish bank Santander had a part in it, but Ferrari was after a leader in the cockpit.

* * *

Alonso joins Ferrari – nine months after the story first broke
30 September 2009

Well, it's finally been confirmed; Fernando Alonso is joining Ferrari next season for three years' initial term. The team has also confirmed that Felipe Massa will be racing for them again.

Formula 1 has its dream scenario, which harks back to the Prost versus Senna days – Hamilton in a McLaren versus Alonso in a Ferrari, two drivers on the same level with some history between them.

F1, like any sport, works at its absolute best when it has a really great rivalry at its core and we now have that. Except that it's even better because Kimi Raikkonen may also join McLaren and he will be out to get Alonso too. Add in a very strong supporting cast of Vettel and Webber in Red Bulls, Button and Rosberg in Brawns and Kubica in a Renault and F1 looks like it has reinvented itself overnight into something utterly un-putdownable.

After all the pain and misery of the off-track politics in 2007, 2008 and 2009, the scene is set for some classic years of racing. Lucky old BBC!

The Alonso-to-Ferrari story first came to light at New Year 2008, when Pino Allievi wrote of it in *Gazzetta dello Sport*. The piece had no quotes nor attributions, was short and to the point. It said that Alonso had an agreement with Ferrari for 2011, but that it might start in 2010 depending on how the year panned out.

I posted on it at the time, saying that Pino has never been wrong in my experience when it comes to Ferrari stories like this. There are all sorts of reasons, but let's just say it's the way things are done in Italy. Lots of people have doubted the report, but Pino hasn't let us down.

It's the right move for Alonso and the team in many ways. Alonso is the leader the team has been lacking since Michael Schumacher retired in 2006. He will fit well alongside Felipe Massa, who is fast enough to push him and beat him, as he did with Schumacher and Raikkonen. It will be interesting to see how Alonso copes with Massa as he will find it hard to make any demands which impact on Massa's chances.

Alonso almost went to Ferrari in 2002. He had agreed a deal with Jean Todt to become the Ferrari test driver (ironically the role Massa then took) in the garden at Todt's villa near Maranello. He was with his then manager Adrian Campos. But soon after he was persuaded by Flavio Briatore to join Renault with the promise of a race seat (Jenson Button's) for 2003.

Alonso had not signed the Ferrari contract and he told Todt he wasn't coming. Todt vowed that he would never drive for Ferrari as long as he was there. Alonso went on to win two world titles with Renault at a time when he would have been second fiddle to Michael Schumacher had he made his original move.

He went to McLaren because, unlike most young racers, a seat at Ferrari was not his childhood dream, whereas one at McLaren was. This is because it was Ayrton Senna's team. But almost as soon as he started there he realised that Ron Dennis was not the person he thought he was and the rest was downhill fast.

When Schumacher was closing in on retirement the only choice for Ferrari to replace him was Kimi Raikkonen, the only obviously supreme driver around at the time. This strong bargaining position gave Raikkonen the financial deal of a lifetime.

Raikkonen won the 2007 title, coming from 17 points behind Lewis Hamilton with two races to go. But the relationship never gelled and he is leaving the team a year ahead of his contract expiry at the end of 2010, a contract extension which he triggered himself in 2008.

Would Alonso have done better than Raikkonen in 2007 and 2008 with the Ferrari? My own view is that he would, but we will never know.

Ferrari's press release is curious; it focuses very respectfully on Raikkonen. It mentions that Alonso and Massa, backed up by Fisichella as third driver will be the team, but the rest of it is about Raikkonen, thanking him for his service. There is a Raikkonen quote, but strangely there is no quote from Alonso about what this moment means.

Raikkonen speaks with great regret about his departure from the team and you can almost hear the lump in his throat. "I am very sad to be leaving a team with which I have spent three fantastic years, during which time I won plenty of races," he said. "Together, we have won 50 per cent of the world titles in that period and I managed to take the drivers' title in 2007, thus achieving the target I had set myself at the start of my career. I have always felt at home with everyone here and I will have many happy memories of my time with the team."

Chapter Ten
October 2009

Domenicali and Raikkonen differ on the reasons why he was dropped
1 October 2009

Today has been a very interesting day in the Suzuka paddock - one of those days when there is a real buzz in the air and some paddock theatre going on.

With the announcement last night of Kimi Raikkonen's removal from Ferrari and Fernando Alonso's arrival, it was clear that their respective press briefings and that of Ferrari boss Stefano Domenicali were going to be interesting.

Kimi looked rather crestfallen today, as you would expect, but he was very dignified in the way he conducted himself in public. He did not criticise the team and they did not criticise him. It is not an easy job to sit in front of the assembled media when you have been dumped by your team. He has said many times in the past that he would end his career at Ferrari, but now he is having to rethink that aim. In doing so he has left himself the option of quitting F1 at the end of the year. He had always rather implied that he would stop when his Ferrari contract expired at the end of 2011.

Meanwhile Alonso looked happy but not triumphant. He spoke with enthusiasm, but judged the tone just right. I'll discuss him in a separate post.

Judging from the comments section on my website, many fans are struggling to understand Ferrari's decision to drop Raikkonen for Alonso, as are a lot of journalists in the F1 paddock. The question kept coming up, phrased differently each time, but always with the same thrust: why do the team feel that Alonso is a better bet than Kimi?

Both Raikkonen and Domenicali were asked this and Raikkonen took the tack of implying that the decision was based on commercial considerations, in other words on the arrival of Santander as a sponsor of Ferrari: "There are many reasons. In F1 there is always a lot of money and there can always be different options. That's what happened in the end. It's nothing to do with racing or what I do in the team."

I have heard rumours that Philip Morris is paying the severance money to Raikkonen and that his salary at McLaren is being paid by Santander, although the numbers doing the rounds for next year's driver salaries are vastly inflated, according to Domenicali.

Raikkonen was then asked how much his departure had to do with the arrival of Santander. He smiled in that involuntary way of his, and the expression on his face spoke volumes, but all he said was, "You'll have to ask the team..." Then there was a pause and he almost said something further, but apparently decided against it.

An hour or so later I said to Domenicali that Raikkonen had implied that the decision to replace him was commercially motivated. He denied this unequivocally. "No, it is not correct that it was a commercial decision." Asked repeatedly why Ferrari thought that Alonso was a better bet than Raikkonen, Domenicali said, "When you have to take the decision you think that the couple of drivers for the future should be the best that it is possible to have."

He made it clear that as boss of the team, the decision had been his, and certainly my Italian colleagues say that Domenicali is the one who pushed very hard for the transfer to be made. He has to think of his own future. After two seasons as team boss he has won one constructors' championship but had a poor year this year. He needs the team to return to the top level and he wants all the elements in place to achieve that.

He also revealed that the team had signed a deal with Alonso for 2011 during the summer, but then because of Renault's problems over the Singapore race-fixing scandal, the possibility arose of bringing him to Ferrari a year early.

As for the risk of holding on to Felipe Massa when it is not yet clear that he will be able to drive, the team is confident that Massa will be back to his usual level, but it seems that they have options anyway. For one thing, Giancarlo Fisichella will be there, should Massa struggle very badly. Beyond that, Robert Kubica looks set to sign a deal for only one year at Renault and would potentially be available for 2011. But

Ferrari do seem convinced that Massa will be back and that he will be every bit as good as he was before his accident.

Raikkonen was clear that although things didn't work out in the end and he would have liked to have won more races, on the whole he was happy with his three years at Ferrari and had no regrets. "I'm happy with what I have done. I think I will still have a good future." He said he wouldn't have changed anything about the decisions made and the contracts signed.

But crucially he then went on to say that he might not even carry on racing. "I haven't decided yet whether I want to race or what I want to do," he said. "I had a contract for next year, now I don't any more. That changes things, so maybe I will race, maybe I will not. There is a chance [he'll do rallies] but there is a chance I'll do Formula One too."

Mosley says Vatanen "will lose badly"
2 October 2009

The Guardian newspaper is reporting that FIA president Max Mosley has sent a stern letter to Prince Feisal, of the Jordanian Royal family, warning that the candidate he supports in the FIA election later this month "will lose and lose badly". Prince Feisal has been nominated by Vatanen as one of his vice-presidents on the sporting side.

The gloves are now well and truly off in the fight to be elected Mosley's successor. The support of Prince Feisal was quite a decisive win for Ari Vatanen and could change the dynamic of the Middle East quite considerably. Mosley is openly supporting the other candidate, Jean Todt.

Prince Feisal has been hosting a conference this week in Amman on the future of motoring and motor sport in the region. Sir Jackie Stewart played a prominent role in the conference, calling for a change of leadership at the top of the FIA. He is very close to the royal family in Jordan; the late King Hussein was godfather to Jackie's son, Paul. Stewart is a long-time and vocal opponent of Mosley.

Mosley's letter warned that Vatanen's recent negative comments about his governance and "autocracy" would divide the FIA membership.

"Any thoughts that after this election everyone in motor sport can unite and work together can now be forgotten. It is not possible to make statements like Vatanen's and then expect the victims of those insults to forget what has been said. The simple fact is that Vatanen will lose the election and lose badly, not least because he chose to denigrate the FIA and those currently in office."

Prince Feisal is quoted in the *Jordan Times* saying, "Jordan has always maintained a strong relationship with the FIA president, so I am deeply disappointed by the content and the insinuations of his letter which have raised serious questions as to the credibility of the upcoming and future elections.

"Jordan was delighted to welcome Max to Jordan for our inaugural World Rally Championship round last year, an event that I am pleased to report will return in 2010," he continued, adding that he also thought that the FIA should have an "ethics commission".

"I strongly propose that proper bidding structures and processes should be introduced for countries wishing to join major championships like Formula One and the WRC, which will further raise the bar in terms of their quality and organisation."

Vettel dominates Suzuka; can he do a Raikkonen and steal the championship?
4 October 2009

Sebastian Vettel drove a totally dominant race to win the Japanese Grand Prix, ahead of Jarno Trulli and Lewis Hamilton. It was Vettel's fourth ever victory and his third of this season.

Vettel maintained the lead gained from pole position, taking a very assertive line into Turn 1 to stop Hamilton, using the KERS on the McLaren to good effect, from passing. Hamilton was able to jump Trulli for second but from then on the Italian drove an incredible race, fighting throughout to get the position back. He achieved it at the second pit stops.

A substantial late accident by Jaime Alguersuari in the Toro Rosso brought out the safety car, which offered Hamilton the chance to attack Trulli again, but his KERS system had malfunctioned and he wasn't able to mount a challenge.

All three drivers were euphoric when they came into the unilateral television interview room after the race. All had thoroughly enjoyed driving flat out on this majestic circuit and Trulli and Hamilton in particular had enjoyed their tense race-long battle. Trulli said it was like "a race of qualifying laps".

The race represented one of Trulli's most impressive performances, as did his lap in qualifying yesterday. Toyota have been making more positive noises this weekend about staying in the sport until 2012 at least and Trulli, like Glock last weekend, has stated his case very clearly for being retained, despite the team's indication that both are free to look elsewhere for a drive.

At one point it looked as though the Brawn team would clinch the Constructors' Championship today, but it didn't quite happen. Rubens Barrichello headed home his team-mate Jenson Button for the third time in the last five races. However Brawn need just one more point to clinch that championship. They thought they might get it when the stewards investigated Nico Rosberg for speeding under the safety car on his way into the pits, but he was cleared of any offence because the "low fuel" indicator overrode the speed/time screen on his dashboard display.

Button was down in 12th place at one point, but fought his way back up once again. He had a stroke of luck when the cars he was following, Adrian Sutil and Heikki Kovalainen, collided. Sutil had been building up to a pass and lunged down the inside into the chicane. He then didn't leave Kovalainen room in the second part of the chicane and was spun around. Button gratefully sailed through to gain two places in the closing stages and caught up with Barrichello, but wasn't able to pass him and the pair ended up seventh and eighth.

So the championship goes on at least to the penultimate round in Brazil. Barrichello is 14 points behind Button with a maximum of 20 available, whilst Vettel has closed the gap to Button down to 16 points, one less than the margin Kimi Raikkonen successfully closed down on Hamilton in 2007.

"Anything can happen and we are here to fight," said Vettel. "The target is to win the next two races and then see what the others can do. If that's good enough to win it, then fine. The next track we know and this year we have a stronger car. Abu Dhabi, it's difficult to know."

As we saw in 2007, anything can happen.

JAPANESE GRAND PRIX
Suzuka 52 laps

1.	Vettel	Red Bull-Renault		1h28:20.443
2.	Trulli	Toyota	+	4.877
3.	Hamilton	McLaren-Mercedes	+	6.472
4.	Raikkonen	Ferrari	+	7.940
5.	Rosberg	Williams-Toyota	+	8.793
6.	Heidfeld	BMW Sauber	+	9.509
7.	Barrichello	Brawn-Mercedes	+	10.641
8.	Button	Brawn-Mercedes	+	11.474

DRIVERS' STANDINGS
1. Button   85
2. Barrichello   71
3. Vettel   69
4. Webber   51.5
5. Raikkonen   45
6. Hamilton   43

CONSTRUCTORS' STANDINGS
1. Brawn-Mercedes   156
2. Red Bull-Renault   120.5
3. Ferrari   67
4. McLaren-Mercedes   65
5. Toyota   54.5
6. Williams-Toyota   34.5

A little pointer as to why Red Bull will be quick in Brazil
6 October 2009

Mark Webber's Japanese Grand Prix looked like a bit of a write-off; he finished last, two laps behind his team-mate who won the race in the same car. But it could turn out to have been a very worthwhile afternoon.

The Australian crashed on Saturday morning, doing enough damage to his car for it to be scrapped, which meant that he had to miss qualifying and start the race from the pit lane.

He was back into the pits twice in the first few laps to fix a loose headrest. From then on his race was a test session: but it appears to have been a very valuable one.

The team had brought a range of front wings with them in the freight. (They have also promised to bring a new one to each of the final two races.) As the race went on, Webber tested out parts for the next race in Brazil and he was using the "Brazil" front wing when he set the fastest lap of the race, 1m 32.569s, shortly after the safety car period.

Looking through the race lap times his long-run pace was not particularly good the rest of the time, but sources say that the team was very encouraged by the results of Webber's 53 lap "test session" - a rare opportunity in Formula 1 these days.

Kubica gives Renault a vote of confidence
7 October 2009

Robert Kubica has brushed aside any concerns over the Renault cheating scandal and has shown his faith in the team by signing for next season. As one of the most highly rated drivers in F1, he had a choice of seats for next year, but he has gone with Renault.

The Pole has been figuring out what would be his best option since BMW's shock announcement of their withdrawal from F1 in July. His manager, Daniele Morelli, is a very smart man and has a good radar for F1 trends and developments.

A month or so ago, I thought Williams was Kubica's first choice but I think he may have been put off lately by the uncertainty about which engine the team intends to use in 2010. The team seems to have cut off discussions with Renault and is now considering Cosworth. This may be part of a wider commercial deal, possibly involving a large company and equity stakes in either Williams or Cosworth (or both) changing hands in the future.

The Renault announcement says that Kubica will drive "from the 2010 season onwards". That is rather vague and my hunch is that he may have done a one-year deal with options, because there are quite a few things which could happen in the driver market for 2011 and he will want to be in a position to capitalise if, for example, Felipe Massa isn't the same driver as he was before his accident or if Raikkonen goes to McLaren for just one year and then retires.

I heard that Kubica signed the deal on Saturday in Japan. It makes sense for both sides; Renault is keen to emerge from the cheating scandal and refresh its sporting brand. It has such a proud history in motor sport, and this latest scandal sits oddly with the past.

The young Pole will be welcomed with open arms by the engineers, who were not happy with Briatore for losing him in 2006 to BMW. Kubica's first test was in a Renault, as a prize for winning the World Series by Renault. He went well, but Briatore delayed, so Morelli parlayed the Renault test into a test and then a race seat with Sauber and BMW. Word had got out about how fast Kubica had been in the Renault test and when Morelli showed Sauber and Mario Theissen the data, Kubica was signed without even testing the BMW Sauber car! The Renault engineers have thought ever since what a great team Alonso and Kubica would have made. The pair are good friends.

Massa gives Alonso an uncomfortable welcome
15 October 2009

Felipe Massa is playing an interesting game at the moment, with regards to his team-mate for next season, Fernando Alonso.

First at a lunch for Brazilian journalists yesterday in São Paulo, he claimed that Alonso must have known about the Singapore crash plot, even though he was cleared of any involvement by the FIA. "Fernando knew," he said. "Of course he knew, I'm one hundred per cent certain of that. In a team it is impossible not to know the strategy of the other driver."

Many of the drivers say the same thing privately, but have not wanted to do so publicly. Massa did speak out and he does not deny that he did, even though he later issued a clarification via the Ferrari website.

"What I've said is the outcome of a hunch I've had and is not based on any concrete evidence," he said. "The FIA World Council announced that there was no indication that Fernando may have been informed of what had happened and I respect this outcome. Obviously I'm very disappointed about what transpired last year in Singapore: I have already said several times what I thought about it and now it's time to close that chapter and to look to the future. What is certain is that this episode will not mar in any way the relationship I'll have with Fernando when we will be team-mates."

Under the circumstances Massa might have been expected to keep his hunches to himself in the interests of team harmony for next year. But it looks as if it isn't going to be that kind of relationship and he isn't going to play that kind of game.

Massa knows that Alonso is a very different prospect as a team-mate from Raikkonen and he knows that many people expect him to lose the inevitable psychological struggle with the Spaniard. McLaren boss Martin Whitmarsh offered Ferrari a piece of advice on how to manage Alonso last week: "I'm sure as long as Fernando is winning everything will be fine."

The move to Ferrari is such a big thing for Alonso and has been so long in the making, that he is sure to try to take control. Massa is fast enough to trouble him and they both know that. The key question is: is Massa strong enough in the head? And that is what we will find out next season. Those close to him say he most definitely is. What's intriguing about Massa's comments here in Brazil is that he clearly wants to demonstrate to Alonso from the outset that he is no pushover and that he has no qualms about probing Alonso's weak points - such as the doubt over his involvement in the crash scandal and thus, by extension, his reputation.

This is great stuff. I love this psychological business between drivers, as it is so fundamental to the racer's instinct and provides such a window on the soul. The key is to play a hard game, but without damaging your own reputation in the process.

Massa also said that if it had been up to him he would have been behind the wheel this weekend in Brazil. "I feel ready to race and if they asked me to I'd take the wheel. But the risks involved in another incident are very high."

I suspect that Massa wanted to race again this season because he wanted to make sure he had his feet back under the table at Ferrari before Alonso's arrival.

Their partnership will make for some great entertainment and is sure to be very successful on the track, but it is crystal clear from this episode that it is going to take some very strong management to keep the Ferrari ship on an even keel.

Webber wins race, Button wins championship in style
18 October 2009

A fantastic Brazilian Grand Prix ended with Red Bull's Mark Webber taking the victory, his second of the season, whilst Jenson Button won the world championship, coincidentally finishing the race in fifth place, the result that did it for Lewis Hamilton last season. Button becomes the tenth British driver to win the F1 world championship.

Robert Kubica finished second having produced the drive of the day and Lewis Hamilton had a storming drive from the back of the grid to finish third.

Brawn won the Constructors' World Championship in their first season as an F1 team. As everyone will remember, the team, formerly Honda, almost didn't survive the winter and was saved at the last minute by Ross Brawn and his management team. To win the world title from that position is certainly fairy-tale stuff. Button needed to sprint, rather than crawl across the finish and he did so today with a tremendous drive.

Starting 14th on the grid, Button was helped greatly by a series of accidents at the start, which brought out the safety car. He was up to ninth at that point, with a long fuel load, and that was the platform for winning the title today. But he had to go out and attack, passing

Grosjean, Nakajima, Kobayashi and Buemi. All were bold moves, of the kind that he has put in all season. After some poor races lately it was just the swashbuckling drive he needed to make himself feel good about clinching the title.

The pass on Kobayashi in particular was really important. The Japanese, on his race debut, proved a stubborn competitor. Button needed to get past him at that particular point as Sebastian Vettel and Lewis Hamilton were threatening from behind and the cars ahead which he needed to pass, like Buemi, were getting away from him.

Rubens Barrichello, Button's main opposition, started from pole position, but after his first pit stop he rejoined in traffic and was passed by Sebastian Vettel. A battle with Lewis Hamilton cost the Brazilian further time and he lost places to Mark Webber and Robert Kubica as a result. He looked set to finish third but a late puncture dropped him down to eighth place.

Vettel, Button's other championship rival, ended up fourth after a strong drive from 15th on the grid.

After a lot of talk recently about whether Button would make a worthy world champion, he was justifiably proud of his drive today and his world crown. "It's amazing, I'm world champion and I think that race deserved it," he said. "That was the way to do it. I had to make it work. Kobayashi was crazy. It took a while to get past him. It's the most amazing day today. After qualifying I felt sick because of how tough it was. The last few months have been stressful. But it was a great race, really enjoyable."

Ross Brawn was in tears after the race. "It will take a while to sink in. It's special. He's [Button] made it hard work the second half of the season. He had a great race today, he knew what he had to do. We have lost a little bit compared to the other teams lately, but he's stuck with it and he deserves it."

I remember so vividly that day in Barcelona in March when this Brawn car appeared on the track and it was so obvious that it was a rocket ship. The opening races of the season went Button's way, he won six times in the first half of the season, but then a combination of the Brawn team losing the development battle against Red Bull and McLaren and

Button making heavy weather of the races, resulted in a pretty stressful situation.

Jenson Button, world champion – get in there!

BRAZILIAN GRAND PRIX
Interlagos 71 laps

1. Webber	Red Bull-Renault		1h32:23.081
2. Kubica	BMW Sauber	+	7.626
3. Hamilton	McLaren-Mercedes	+	18.944
4. Vettel	Red Bull-Renault	+	19.652
5. Button	Brawn-Mercedes	+	29.005
6. Raikkonen	Ferrari	+	33.340
7. Buemi	Toro Rosso-Ferrari	+	35.991
8. Barrichello	Brawn-Mercedes	+	45.454

DRIVERS' STANDINGS

1. Button   89
2. Vettel   74
3. Barrichello   72
4. Webber   61.5
5. Hamilton   49
6. Raikkonen   48

CONSTRUCTORS' STANDINGS

1. Brawn-Mercedes   161
2. Red Bull-Renault   135.5
3. McLaren-Mercedes   71
4. Ferrari   70
5. Toyota   54.5
6. Williams-Toyota   34.5

Button: "That was the best race of my life"
18 October 2009

Jenson Button has shouted himself hoarse with celebrating his world championship victory and giving endless interviews.

He claims that today's race was the best of his career to date."This was my best race I've driven in my life, I know because of the emotion that's involved in it, but also because I knew what I had to do – I did it, and that is why I am sitting up here as world champion," he said. "I am going to enjoy this moment very much. The people around me have been so supportive. I might have come across like I don't care about this in the past, but that was just me keeping a face. It shows a weakness if you show it is hurting or stressful, but I can say it now, it was a very tough few months and I needed the people around me, especially the team to fight for this.

"Today I didn't win the race but I did the best I could with the car and it felt like a win to me. I am the WORLD CHAMPION – and I am not going to stop saying it!"

Button admitted that he had made life difficult for himself in recent races, not least because of his uncertain qualifying form. "Qualifying has been something I couldn't get my head around for the last few races," he said. "I don't know what it is, but it is something that we need to look at for the next race. I don't want to be beaten in the next race as the world champion. Maybe it is the stress of it all, maybe it's just that we haven't got it together. I think it's probably the latter."

Certainly at the same time and in the same car, Rubens Barrichello was getting it together and putting Button's championship lead under threat.

Ross Brawn made a reference to Button making hard work of it recently and it's interesting to hear Button admit that maybe the stress and pressure got to him a little bit. He was definitely edgy before the podium result in Monza, which steadied the nerves a bit, but he kept getting himself into trouble in qualifying, which gave him too much to do in the races. He relied on the bad luck of his rivals through that time and after qualifying it looked like he might be in trouble again. But there is always a strong chance of either rain or a safety car in Brazil to give you a chance to make things happen and today he got a safety car.

He must feel a huge sense of relief above anything else that he has not thrown it away. Today's race winner, Mark Webber, summed up a rival's perspective on Button's recent state of mind: "I think he will sleep better now, because he's been incredibly nervous, there's no question about that," he said. "He's been absolutely bricking himself the last few weeks."

Another strong result today for Webber's team-mate Sebastian Vettel moved him into second place in the championship and he can look back at the opportunities he had to win the title. Of the races he has finished this year Vettel has had a higher points average than Button. The crashes and reliability issues are what cost him the title.

Button admitted that there were points in his career when he thought he might not ever be champion, not least when it dawned on him in his second season in F1 with the Benetton team that he wasn't mature enough to handle Formula 1.

Ironically, given what has happened this year with Nelson Piquet, Button was struggling at the Renault team in 2002 and was dropped by Flavio Briatore, his then team boss. David Richards hired him for BAR (allegedly against the advice of Bernie Ecclestone) and that started a relationship which has had many ups and downs but has culminated in today's success. Button's string of podiums in 2004 and the win in 2006 cemented his belief that he had what it takes to win in F1, he just needed the team to give him the car to do it in. He got that car this year.

"I suppose my second year in F1 was the toughest personally," he said, reflecting on his low point of lack of belief. "After my first year it wasn't enjoyable. It was enjoyable at Williams and got great results, but I really didn't work hard enough. Basically I was too inexperienced and too young to be racing. The second and third years of my career were very difficult, especially my second. That is when I knew it wasn't just speed, you can't win races with just that. You need to work on many different areas and F1 becomes your life. That was the most difficult season."

Todt wins a landslide: major changes on the way for F1
23 October 2009

Max Mosley is no longer the president of the FIA.

Jean Todt has been elected to the role, with a landslide majority. This will mean some major changes in the structure of the body that regulates the F1 world championship.

In the end Todt received almost three times the amount of votes as his rival, Ari Vatanen. Todt had 135 backers, with Vatanen on 49 and there were 12 abstentions.

Todt will make some immediate changes, the consequences of which will be felt before the start of the next F1 season. He plans to introduce an F1 commissioner to oversee the FIA's role in the sport, dealing with the teams, with Bernie Ecclestone and with the rule-making process. Todt is set to keep himself at arm's length from the sport. With the election out of the way, attention will now focus on who that F1 commissioner will be.

The new president also plans to strengthen up the stewards, who have been the centre of some controversy in recent years. It remains to be seen whether Mosley's trusted deputy, Alan Donnelly, will retain his role. Rumours during the Japanese Grand Prix weekend suggested that he might not. Perhaps he is hoping for the F1 commissioner's role? How much of a regime change are we likely to see?

There was a swift reaction to Todt's victory from the teams. FOTA president Luca di Montezemolo, said: "I would like to send my best wishes to Jean Todt in his new role, as I have always appreciated his ability, dedication and commitment. I am sure that, under his guidance, the Federation will be rejuvenated and will restore a climate open to dialogue and constructive collaboration with the teams and FOTA, thus ensuring stability of the regulations and the whole environment."

Todt was a divisive figure when he ran Ferrari. However many of the people Todt clashed with in the past are no longer in F1, for example Ron Dennis and Flavio Briatore. But Frank Williams is still there and he has been close to the FIA under the recent Mosley regime. It will be fascinating to see how that relationship works. Toyota's John Howett was less than enthusiastic about the idea of a Todt presidency over the summer, one of few F1 team principals to express a view on this subject.

Although Howett didn't mention Todt by name, he said that the FIA should elect someone "independent". Today Howett welcomed Todt with these words: "I am convinced that Jean Todt's presidency represents an opportunity for all Formula One's stakeholders to unite under his leadership and work together to strengthen our sport."

Chapter Eleven
November 2009

The final race of the season was at the new Yas Marina Circuit in Abu Dhabi. The facility was built on a no-expense spared basis and it is unlikely we will see anything like it again. The track is the centrepiece of a $22 billion development programme to turn Yas Island and the next door Saddiyat Island into entertainment, culture and tourism hubs for the 21st century. Unlike some other recent additions to the F1 calendar, this circuit is no white elephant.

Behind the scenes there was a lot of business being done which would continue to shape the Formula 1 of the future. Mercedes main board was there to finalise details of the deal to buy Brawn GP via its Abu Dhabi-based shareholder. Ron Dennis was back in the paddock for the first time since the lying scandal in Malaysia, new FIA president Jean Todt was there, as were the leading figures from CVC. Ferrari's top management made the trip too, to meet with their Abu Dhabi-based shareholders. The giant Ferrari World, set to be the world's largest indoor theme park, when it opens next year, dominated the skyline around the track.

There was a strong feeling of renewal in the air. After a revolutionary year in which the sport had almost destroyed itself there was the hum of serious business going on as the cars lapped the new circuit.

* * *.

Super Vettel lights up Abu Dhabi
1 November 2009

Sebastian Vettel won the first Abu Dhabi Grand Prix today, his fourth win of the season and the sixth for his Red Bull Racing team. Teammate Mark Webber finished second, fighting off a late challenge from Jenson Button in the Brawn-Mercedes.

Not only was this Vettel's fourth win of the season but it was also the fourth one-two finish for Red Bull Racing and, encouragingly for them, they have won the final three races of the season, which bodes well for 2010. Red Bull has become a top team this season and they believe that they can stay there for the future. This result gives Vettel second place in the Drivers' Championship.

Lewis Hamilton started from pole position and led the opening stint, but was troubled with a brake problem from early on. He was unable to build a big enough lead to combat Vettel's longer fuel strategy and lost the lead to the German. Shortly afterwards he was told to pit and retire the car. Abnormal brake wear was the reason.

In the middle section of the race, Vettel pulled away easily from team-mate Mark Webber, meanwhile Jenson Button had another battle with Kamui Kobayashi as he emerged from his first stop.

The Japanese was on light fuel at the time and attacked the world champion very aggressively, forcing Button into a mistake under braking into Turn 8. It was a stunning piece of driving by Kobayashi. Button said after their battle in Brazil that Kobayashi is "crazy" and clearly was mindful of that during this latest skirmish.

Kobayashi was on a one-stop strategy and was fighting Button for a podium, but when he switched to the soft tyre for his second stint his pace dropped off. Still he came in a creditable sixth.

In the closing stages of the race Webber was struggling with the soft tyre and Button harried him relentlessly, but Webber was able to hold him off.

Meanwhile in the battle for third place in the Constructors' Championship Kimi Raikkonen lost out to Heikki Kovalainen in the pit stops. The race had some overtaking, largely due to lighter cars on different strategies from heavier cars which had just pitted. But the field spread out a lot in the opening stint and the retirement of Hamilton cost the race its incisive edge until the final cameo from Webber and Button.

ABU DHABI GRAND PRIX
Yas Marina 55 laps

1. Vettel	Red Bull-Renault	1h34:03.314	
2. Webber	Red Bull-Renault	+	17.857
3. Button	Brawn-Mercedes	+	18.467
4. Barrichello	Brawn-Mercedes	+	22.735
5. Heidfeld	BMW Sauber	+	26.253
6. Kobayashi	Toyota	+	28.343
7. Trulli	Toyota	+	34.366
8. Buemi	Toro Rosso-Ferrari	+	41.294

FINAL DRIVERS' STANDINGS

1. Button	95	11. Kovalainen	22
2. Vettel	84	12. Massa	22
3. Barrichello	77	13. Heidfeld	19
4. Webber	69.5	14. Kubica	17
5. Hamilton	49	15. Fisichella	8
6. Raikkonen	48	16. Buemi	6
7. Rosberg	34.5	17. Sutil	5
8. Trulli	32.5	18. Kobayashi	3
9. Alonso	26	19. Bourdais	2
10. Glock	24		

FINAL CONSTRUCTORS' STANDINGS

1. Brawn-Mercedes	172	6. BMW Sauber	36
2. Red Bull-Renault	153.5	7. Williams-Toyota	34.5
3. McLaren-Mercedes	71	8. Renault	26
4. Ferrari	70	9. Force India-Mercedes	13
5. Toyota	59.5	10.Toro Rosso-Ferrari	8

F1 finds a new hero in Kobayashi
1 November 2009

For the second race in a row, Kamui Kobayashi set the place alight with some bold driving, giving the lie to the theory that F1 is too tough for rookie drivers.

Starting his second Grand Prix in 12th place, he was the second best placed of the cars on a one-stop strategy today, after Kimi Raikkonen, but he finished well ahead of the Ferrari driver. His strategy brought him into contact with Jenson Button again.

Today they came into contact just after Button's first stop on lap 17. At this point Kobayashi had another 13 laps to go until his stop, so the difference in fuel weight between the two cars was 12 laps, worth about a second per lap. Kobayashi had a go and Button outbraked himself trying to hold him off.

"The first big stop is turn eight and when you have got that much fuel on board it is always very difficult to judge the braking point," said Button. "I slightly outbraked myself and locked the rears and the fronts and ran a bit wide and he got past. In reality it didn't make a difference to my race as he was quicker than me at that point."

His analysis of the incident showed that Button still wasn't able to shake off the mentality of protecting a championship lead, rather than going for it, even though the championship was over. Kobayashi had nothing to lose and so was able to fight his ground without inhibition.

At that stage both men had one more pit stop to make. Button was being told by his race engineer Andrew Shovlin that Kobayashi was the guy he was racing against. By the time the Japanese made his stop on lap 30 he was seven seconds ahead of Button. At this point he switched to the soft tyre. He lost 17 seconds to Button over the next 12 laps, mainly because it took him a few laps to settle into a rhythm on the soft tyre. Button pushed very hard in this phase and when the Englishman made his second stop on lap 42 he emerged 10 seconds ahead of Kobayashi.

Tonight Toyota boss John Howett pretty much implied that Kobayashi had done enough in his two races to secure the seat for next season – provided that the Toyota main board votes to stay in the sport at its crunch meeting on 15 November. "It looks like it," he said. "We will have to give really serious consideration, as he has shown very good strong results.

"I am very impressed. We were very happy again. What we like is his real fighting spirit. He is not intimidated by anybody. It's very positive."

I had a chat with Kobayashi on Friday and as he used his hands to illustrate how he had positioned his car relative to Button's in Brazil, I noticed that he has a tattoo on his right wrist, which he covers up with a leather bracelet. It is hard to see exactly what the tattoo says, but the first two characters are "F1". On his other wrist is the blingiest Breitling watch I have ever seen.

Kobayashi has made a very positive impression; he's a fighter, he's clearly quick and if he can find consistency in qualifying and a bit more pace at the beginning of a stint after a pit stop, he might well turn out to be a real diamond.

Toyota follow Honda, BMW and Bridgestone out of F1
4 November 2009

It has been a tough week for Japanese involvement in F1. Following on from Bridgestone's announcement that they will withdraw at the end of 2010, Toyota have confirmed the news that many people have been expecting throughout the season; they are pulling out of F1 with immediate effect.

This opens up a place on the Formula 1 grid for the Sauber team, which BMW sold to Qadbak. As things stand there will be 13 teams next season, only three of whom are manufacturer backed. F1 has lost half its manufacturers within the last 12 months.

The balance within F1 will now change quite dramatically, as the influence of the manufacturers diminishes and more independent teams come through. Only Mercedes, Renault and Ferrari are left now. Mercedes are in the early stages of a shift away from McLaren and on to Brawn, making the new world champion team look a very strong package for the future.

Toyota's withdrawal is no great surprise, despite recent claims from team boss John Howett that they would stay the course. The company is making huge losses as the global car market collapses and even this time last year a pullout was anticipated, but Toyota were pre-empted by Honda. It had been suggested that a decision would be taken on 15 November, but the company's president said this morning that the company would end its involvement, after eight seasons in which there were eight podiums but no wins.

Akio Toyoda said the decision was "unavoidable".

"Since last year with the worsening economic climate, we have been struggling with the question of whether to continue in F1," he said. "We are pulling out of Formula 1 completely. I offer my deepest apologies to Toyota's many fans for not being able to achieve the results we had targeted."

A few hours later Toyota issued a statement:

"TMC, which had viewed its participation in F1 as contributing to the prosperity of automotive culture, remained dedicated to competing at the pinnacle of motor sports, even in the face of the abrupt economic changes that started last year.

"However, when considering TMC's motor-sports activities next year and beyond from a comprehensive mid-term viewpoint reflecting the current severe economic realities, TMC decided to withdraw from F1."

Ironically the move comes as the cost of racing is coming right down, due to the Resource Restriction Agreement, a process Toyota played a part in. The team has spent billions over the last ten years during F1's most expensive period ever. The team's budget was amongst the highest in the sport, with a contribution from Toyota of $300 million after sponsorship and TV money.

Even though the costs are coming down dramatically, this move shows that for a company to be seen to be spending money to go racing when factories are on reduced capacity is unacceptable. This begs the question about Renault's ongoing involvement. The team finished 8th in the championship this year, its worst result since it returned to F1 in 2002 and it lost most of its sponsors after being convicted of race fixing. This is also making it hard for the team to find new sponsors. Renault has weathered the storm so far and decided to carry on in F1. But for how long?

Toyota's move leaves Jarno Trulli and Kamui Kobayashi looking for a drive. Timo Glock is believed to have signed for Renault. Trulli is known to be on the shortlist of Mike Gascoyne at Lotus, but at this stage of his career would probably prefer to work with an existing team rather than a start-up. That said, it may be his only option.

Kobayashi may well have done enough in his two races at the end of the season to get a break with another team. He put on a spirited performance and showed that he has the capacity to be a favourite with the fans.

It really is a buyer's market for drivers at the moment, with many seats still open, but even more drivers looking for work.

* * *

And so a season, which began under a cloud with Honda's withdrawal and the bite of recession, ends with another heavy blow.

Toyota's commitment to F1 had long been questioned, but Bridgestone's announcement took everyone by surprise. It was partly motivated by the economic climate, but also by the law of diminishing returns. As sole tyre supplier it was hard to get positive media coverage for the products and with no-one else to beat there was no "challenging spirit" so beloved by Japanese managers.

Formula 1 ends 2009 with mixed feelings. The sport has survived 2009 rather than prospered through it. A cataclysm was averted in the summer, when the teams' breakaway was called off, but a lot of damage was done by that episode and by the Renault race fixing scandal.

Despite big shows of strength like Abu Dhabi, F1's self esteem has been diminished in 2009 and it will be the job of FOTA, the new FIA president Jean Todt and Bernie Ecclestone to restore it when we all meet again in Bahrain in March 2010.

Index

Index

Index

Index

Index

Index